W9-CFQ-683

Parent Talk Essentials

How to Talk to Kids about Divorce, Sex, Money, School and Being Responsible in Today's World

**Chick Moorman and
Thomas Haller**

Personal Power Press
Merrill, Michigan

Parent Talk Essentials

How to Talk to Kids about Divorce, Sex, Money, School and Being Responsible in Today's World

© 2011 by Chick Moorman, Thomas Haller and
Personal Power Press

Library of Congress Catalogue Card Number: 2010934418

ISBN 978-0-9821568-3-4

All rights reserved. Printed in the United States of America. No part
of this publication may by reproduced, stored in a retrieval system,
or transmitted in any form or by any means, electronic, mechanical,
photocopying, recording or otherwise, without the written
permission of the publisher.

Printed in the United States of America

Personal Power Press
P.O. Box 547, Merrill, MI 48637

Cover Design
Zachary Parker, zdp431@gmail.com

Book Design
Connie M. Thompson, graphicsetc@hughes.net

Cartoons
Martha Campbell

TABLE OF CONTENTS

Relationships

School

Money Talk

INTRODUCTION

How do I talk to my kids about sex? What do I say and at what age do I say it?

I need to tell my kids I'm getting remarried. Is there a best way to communicate that to them?

I knew nothing about money concepts when I was growing up. My parents hid that information from me. I want my kids to develop a healthy money consciousness. How do I make sure that happens?

Is there a best time to tell my kids about the pending divorce? I don't want them to be devastated. Help. I want my children to grow up having positive relationships. What Parent Talk can I use to help them pick worthwhile friends?

Above all else, I want my son and daughter to take personal responsibility for their own lives. I don't want them to assume the victim stance and blame others for what they create in their lives. What can I say to help them be responsible for their actions, behaviors, feelings, and the outcomes they produce?

Getting a good education is important. I want my kids to take school seriously, yet I don't want to nag at them about homework and other school issues. What do I say and how do I communicate my concerns about the importance of school success?

These questions and others like them are asked regularly at many of the parenting workshops we present around the world. The concerned parents who pose them have often read one or more of our previously published books and are familiar with our emphasis on teaching parents effective verbal skills to use with their children. They recognize that to raise responsible, caring, confident children they will need these verbal skills.

Yes, there is a link between the words you speak and the attitudes, beliefs, and outcomes children create in their lives. How you talk to your children matters. The words you use matter. Your style of speaking matters. *Parent Talk Essentials* will help you determine the Parent Talk that matters in the important areas of Divorce, Sex, Money, School, Relationships, and Personal Responsibility. It offers an indepth examination of the practical, workable verbal skills that are needed to help children grow into emotionally healthy, fully functioning young adults in these six essential areas.

In *Parent Talk Essentials* you will find help in

developing the verbal skills that will allow you to communicate effectively in real-life parenting situations. These skills will help you help your children live more productive, guilt-free, rewarding lives. The skills work if you work the skills. Stay conscious. Listen to how you talk to your children. Reflect on your style of speaking from time to time. Decide what you like and what you don't like about your Parent Talk. Implement the ideas that make sense to you. You will recognize them by the feelings they generate inside of you. Trust those feelings, whether they tell you to put the book down or implement the ideas you just read immediately.

Read *Parent Talk Essentials* from front to back. Or jump in at a place you find most timely right now. You decide which sections, which Parent Talk phrases, which words and ideas resonate with your beliefs and the goals you have for your family.

To all the parents who have e-mailed us or spoken up at seminars, saying, "Give us more," we thank you. Thank you for your encouragement, your persistence, and your desire to expand your learning. You have helped call this book into being.

Parent Talk Essentials is finished. That you are holding it in your hands is no accident. You and *Parent Talk Essentials* have come together for a reason. You will find that reason in the pages that follow.

Enjoy.

Chick Moorman and Thomas Haller

PERSONAL RESPONSIBILITY

Raising a responsible young adult, one who can function effectively in today's world, does not happen by luck, coincidence, or magic. It occurs only when parents set out to make it happen by working diligently and purposefully throughout a child's life to see that he or she learns about independence, responsibility, and personal power. It happens where and when parents work intentionally to make themselves dispensable in a child's life.

Not many parents set out to raise a thirty-year-old electronic game player who sprawls on the couch all day sucking up pizza and diet Pepsi. Yet many parents actually subvert their positive intention to raise responsible, confident, fully functioning children. They do it by unconsciously using Parent Talk that allows and encourages helplessness.

What about your Parent Talk? Is it based on language that builds autonomy, independence, and self-responsibility? Or does it consist largely of words and phrases that teach your children dependence? You can find out in this chapter.

Believe that making yourself dispensable is your main job as a parent. If you believe that your job is to be needed, that your central role is to *do for* your children, you will have a difficult time implementing the ideas that follow.

Helping doesn't always help. Sometimes it creates learned helplessness. When you *do for* your children the things they can do for themselves, you are overfunctioning. Overfunctioning begins with the belief: My children need me to *do for* them. Change that belief to: My job is to help my children *do for* themselves.

If you hear yourself saying, "I'll do it," "Here, I can fix it," or any variation of "Let me do it," beware. If you do for, do for, do for, children won't learn to do for themselves. This creates dependence. The most important thing you can do for your children is nothing–nothing they can do for themselves.

"IT'S MY WEEK TO BE RESPONSIBLE FOR THE CLASS PLANT."

"Let me show you how."

Showing is different than *doing for*. It is modeling. It is teaching. It does not take over and usurp the child's responsibility. *Showing* stops way short of completion. It allows the child to do most of the task at hand. It allows the child to finish. It allows the child to feel the rush of accomplishment.

Show your children how to set the table, feed the dog, put their socks on, and mow the grass. You cannot hit a baseball or ride a bike for another person. You can only show them how. You can, however, do laundry for your teenager, tie your child's shoes, button his coat, and fix all his meals. Not good ideas.

We know parents of teenagers who do all their laundry for them. This is not effective parenting. It is overfunctioning. These are *do-for* parents who invite their children to become dependent and helpless and to develop feelings of entitlement.

Your job as a parent in regard to laundry is to teach your children how to do it themselves. Teach the young ones how to put dirty clothes in the laundry closet, down the laundry shoot, or in the hamper. Later they can learn to fold clean laundry and put it away in the proper place in their bedroom. Still later, they can help you sort out the laundry by colors and watch you put it in the machine. Eventually, you can teach your children to measure amounts of soap, set the water level, and adjust the water temperature. By the time they are teenagers they could be doing all their own laundry.

"There is laundry to do. Come on, I'll show you the next step" is effective Parent Talk if your goal is to raise a responsible, independent child. Remember, your job is to teach them how. Their job is to do it.

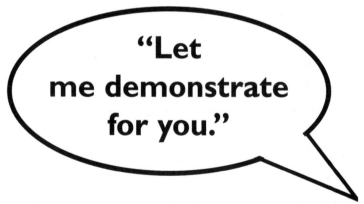

"Let me demonstrate for you."

Alejandro Gomez left his brand new baseball glove out in the rain. When he found it, he brought it in to dry. Once dried, his leather glove, formerly soft and pliable, was now stiff and inflexible. Not exactly what a ten-year-old shortstop needs to have on his hand when fielding ground balls.

Mr. Gomez, after listening to his son's complaints about the stiff glove, came to the rescue. No, he did not rescue by providing a new replacement glove. Nor did he loan Alejandro his personal baseball glove. Replacing the glove would not have helped his son learn about the importance of taking care of his possessions. That would have effectively prevented him from experiencing the natural outcome of not keeping his prized belonging in a safe place.

Instead, Mr. Gomez brought home a small can of Neatsfoot oil. "Let me demonstrate how this works," he told his son. Mr. Gomez then rubbed the oil on the thumb area of the glove. He worked it in slowly with steady pressure. When he had finished making the thumb soft, close to its original condition, he turned to his son. "Feel that," he said. "Notice how soft it is."

"Wow," remarked Alejandro. "It's almost like new." "Yep," said his father. "That's what you have to do if you want a soft glove. If you decide you want to soften it, please do it right here on the old newspapers. I'll be in the living room if you have any questions." With that, the young baseball player's father turned and left the room.

Whether Alejandro chooses to use the oil to soften his glove or not isn't important. What matters is that this father was not confused about roles. He knew precisely what his role was and what it wasn't. Mr. Gomez's job was to teach his son a system for fixing the glove. It was his son's responsibility to use the system. "I'll get you started. You do the rest," "I'll do the first one and then you can take over," and similar Parent Talk is an invitation to the child to finish the task. It is an invitation, not a demand. Let your child be in charge of whether or not the invitation is accepted.

"I'll get that down. It's messy."

"Let me pour it."

"Give it to me. I don't want any on the floor."

If children don't get opportunities to handle messy situations, they seldom improve. Yes, experience can be messy. Pouring your own milk, drinking from a regular cup, adding sprinkles to cookies, and cleaning out the inside of a pumpkin could be real messy. Allow them to learn from experience.

We're not talking about allowing a four-year-old to use a sharp knife on a pumpkin. Of course, it is important to consider health and safety issues and exert control when appropriate. But once health and safety is handled, remember that the more you function, the less your child has to.

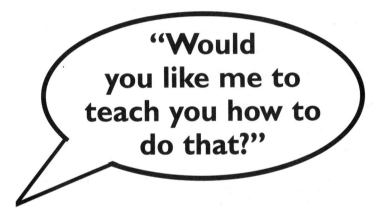

"Would you like me to teach you how to do that?"

This Parent Talk allows children to determine whether or not they want help. It empowers them by giving them control over whether or not they want assistance. If they do, teaching them is more helpful than doing for them.

"Let's practice our escape route if there's a fire."

"I'll be Grandma. You be you. Let's role-play how your apology might go."

"Show me again the way we respectfully communicate anger in our family."

"You take the role of your boyfriend. I'll play your role. Let's see how saying NO looks and sounds one more time."

Do you expect your children to *just say no*, figure out an escape route when a fire engulfs your home, or communicate anger effectively without any practice? If so, you're engaging in wishful thinking. It won't happen. Not anymore than they'll improve hitting a baseball, playing the flute, or reading the printed word without practice.

There are times when it's important to be assertive. Have you taught your children how and supervised their practice? If an adult is invading their space or saying something that's bringing up uncomfortable feelings, they need to know how to be confident and firm. Teach them to speak up for themselves. Give them the words to use. "Leave me alone" or "Stay away from me" work well in these situations. Have them practice being assertive with you.

"Ask me if you would like help."

Many children do not know how to ask for help because they never have to. Parents, teachers, caregivers, and other adults often rush in with help before the child has articulated a desire for that help. Why would a child ever need to ask for help if help always arrives without asking?

Teaching your children to ask for help begins with allowing them to struggle with an issue like cutting their own meat, zipping their coat, or doing math homework. When frustration occurs, respond with, "Looks like you're getting frustrated. Let me know if you'd like some help."

With young children it's important to teach

them specific asking words. Tell them to say, "I want help," or "Help, please." When they see that help arrives after using the appropriate words, they learn to use the words to obtain the desired result.

An important step in developing personal responsibility is learning to ask for help. If you help before your children ask, they won't have a reason to learn how to ask.

"She's feeling a little shy today."

We recently overheard a conversation where a friend approached a parent and child and spoke to the child, asking her a direct question: "How are you doing today, Maria?" The mother responded for the child, replying, "She's not in a very good mood today." The silent message the parent delivered to the child was: "You don't have to speak up for yourself. I will take care of you."

Refrain from answering for your child if you want her to develop her own voice.

When the doctor asks, "Why are you here

today?", when the neighbor inquires, "What was your favorite birthday present?", or when Grandma wants to know, "How do you like school this year?", stay out of it. Allow your child to answer for herself.

"I'll talk to your mother and see if I can get her to change her mind."

Whose relationship with the mother is involved here, yours or the child's? Teach children to solve their own problems. Do not say, "Don't say anything to your mother. I'll handle it for you. I know your mother well, and I can catch her in a good mood."

Say instead, "You're going to have to handle this with your mother. Let me tell you what I know. I generally try to catch her in the afternoon because she gets real busy in the morning. If she's having a bad hair day, forget it. Also, she responds better if you make it sound like a suggestion rather than a demand. Hopefully, these tips will help. I know you can handle it." This style of speaking announces to your child that you believe in him and that you see him as capable.

"I'll send your teacher (coach, boss, Girl Scout leader, choir director) a note and get her to give you more time." This is a classic rescue. Your children will learn a more valuable lesson if you allow them to experience consequences.

If your child is old enough and skilled enough and won't call the store himself, he doesn't want the item badly enough to have it. If he doesn't know how to call the store, teach him to use a phone book or the Internet to find the number. With young children, invite them to sit next to you while they watch you look up the number and make the call. Once again, your job is to teach them a system. Eventually, it will be their job to use it.

"Never talk to strangers" is a slogan often used by parents today. The motivation is to alert their kids to the fact that strangers can do a lot of hurtful things to children and if they just stay away from strangers they will be OK. This flies in the face of the statistics that show many youngsters are molested, abused, and even killed by people they know, often relatives.

But suppose that your child is lost at an amusement park or in a mall, where everyone around her is a stranger? If she can't talk to strangers, who does she turn to? No one. Do you want her wandering around scared and alone until she reconnects with you? Even if it takes several hours? Probably not.

Instead, teach your children how to recognize the people who are most likely to help. That person might be a stranger. Help them learn to look for the helpers.

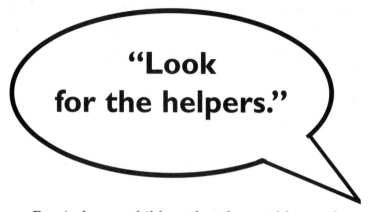

"Look for the helpers."

Remind your children that the world is a place where most people love children and that helpers are everywhere. When you're at the mall or grocery store, point out the people who are likely to help: a woman at the door, a grandmother, a person at the information center. Statistics indicate that women are more likely to take a child who needs help to the appropriate person. Men will often point the child in the right direction but let them navigate the route on their own.

Ask your children as you walk through the mall together, "Who would you turn to if you got lost?" Ask them to explain their reasoning. Debrief with them, discussing their choices and why they made them. Give them practice at using and trusting their intuition. Do not make them wrong for their choices.

When a tragedy occurs such as a hurricane or earthquake, point out the helpers. Helpers always come. Show them the various organizations and charities–police personnel, firefighters, Red Cross members–who are on the ground making people's lives more tolerable regardless of their circumstances.

Use your words to paint a picture of hope rather than fear. We want our children to see that safety exists all around them. When children see the world as safe instead of scary, they are better able to sense an unsafe situation when one arises. If everything is seen as scary, rotten, or hurtful, then the next scary incident that comes along is just like all the others and seems normal.

"No candy until I hear the magic word."

"You know the magic word: Pleeeeeease."

Please do not teach your child that *please* is the magic word. Guess what? Child abductors use the magic word, too. They can be extremely polite until they achieve their prime objective.

Thomas recently overheard a mother instructing her young child to "use the magic word." His ears perked up at the instruction. He listened closely as the mother continued to direct the child, telling him, "I won't give you a piece of gum unless you say please." The child immediately replied, "Pleeeeease, can I have a piece of gum?" The addition of "please" worked. Mom promptly reached in her purse and presented gum to the child, just like magic.

Wow, what an incredible lesson. Many parents use the magic word instruction as a way to teach children to be polite. We agree that children need to be taught how to use "please" and "thank you," as well as table manners, how to interrupt, and even to hold open a door for another person. These are all valuable lessons in social interaction and politeness.

But using the concept of a magic word has a hidden message that teaches a dangerous lesson. Is it true that saying please automatically or magically produces the desired result for the one using it? No. But when we position it as such, we suggest that one must comply with the request simply because the word please was used.

Drop the entire concept of the magic word from your Parent Talk. Instead, say to your children, "It's polite to use the word please when asking for something you want. There is no guarantee that saying please will get you what you want. Sometimes the answer will be yes and sometimes no. But people are more open to responding kindly when they hear words like please and thank you. Can you state your question again using the word please and see what happens?"

As you continue to teach your children to use please in this way, they will learn that they, too, can say, "No, thank you," to a request that is accompanied by a "please." The "magic" of the word is removed and the decision to comply remains with the one who is being asked. This is a necessary strength our children need to have and learn to use appropriately.

"What do you think they want from us?"

When you see someone in the supermarket passing out free samples, ask your children, "What do you think they want from us?" When free soap samples come in the mail, ask your children why the manufacturers sent them. Discuss their possible ulterior motives. Teach your child the danger signal of people bearing gifts. Ice cream, candy, and video games are good bribes. Help your child see them as warning signs of a motivation on the part of the gift giver that may not be in his or her best interest.

"That looks unsafe."

When you see a situation that is potentially unsafe, point it out to your children. Talk about what is unsafe about it and what could be done to make it safe. Tell them why you parked under the light in the parking lot as night approached. Explain why you moved away from the curb as you walked along the sidewalk on a busy or icy street. Talk about why it's not safe to help someone find their lost dog or cat.

Teach your children to give situations the "tummy test." Ask them, "What feels unsafe here?", as you walk down a country road, explore an old barn, or hike in the mountains. Ask them to "check it out inside" as they swing in the park, bicycle through a new neighborhood, or walk through the county fair. Give them opportunities to practice using their intuition.

If a person or situation feels unsafe or scary in their tummy, teach younger children to run. Logic is not important here. Intuition and inner knowing are. Help your children develop this wise part within. Teach them to trust it. Practice so that the skill is present if they ever need it.

More information on children developing their inner authority is included in our book *The 10 Commitments: Parenting with Purpose.* The seventh commitment teaches parents, teachers, and caregivers how to help children develop their inner authority, the only authority they take with them everywhere they go. www.personalpowerpress.com.

"**Complete the cycle.**"

Teach your children to complete the cycle. Everything has a cycle. A tadpole, decaying forest, compost pile, acorn, and all living things have a life cycle. Dishes have a cycle. They begin on the shelf, go to the table, have food placed on them, go to the sink, get cleaned off, get dried, and return to the shelf.

If the coat comes off the hook in the morning and is taken to school, it needs to be returned from school and placed back on the hook. That completes the cycle. "Tevi, please complete the cycle" is more effective Parent Talk than "Pick up your coat" or "Forgetting something?"

Children can complete the cycle by putting their bike back in the garage, returning dinner dishes to the kitchen, and returning tools to their proper place after tightening a loose screw.

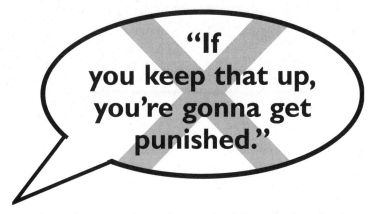

"**If you keep that up, you're gonna get punished.**"

Punishment doesn't work. Not if developing personal responsibility in your child is what you're after.

Yes, punishment may get a quick response in a specific instance. Yet, it is the consistent implementation of reasonable, related consequences that produces long-term behavior change in children. With punishment, children are more likely to focus on you, your behavior, or your anger than on themselves and the results of the choices they made. Punishment rarely produces learning because children are too busy feeling resentment, resistance, and reluctance. They're more likely to spend their time thinking of revenge fantasies and how not to get caught next time than they are about the cause and effect relationship between their behavior and the consequences that followed.

"**This is going to hurt me more than it hurts you.**"

More than one generation of parents has uttered this piece of Parent Talk. It has been delivered by mothers as well as by fathers. It has been spoken calmly and with intense anger. Regardless of its tone, volume, or intensity, it is usually followed by a spanking.

Don't look now, but the familiar adage "This is going to hurt me more than it hurts you" may be true.

Since it's the child's bottom that gets stung, it appears at first glance that the child is the one who gets hurt. Clearly, an adult hand can tolerate more violence than a child's tender backside can. There is no doubt that spanking children hurts them in many ways. Children who are spanked regularly can hurt as much on the inside as they do on the outside. Some of the psychological scars inflicted by hitting children can take years to heal. And yet the supposition remains: Maybe spanking a child *does* hurt the parent as much or more than it hurts the child.

When a spanking occurs, the child disconnects. He withdraws emotionally from the parent and the situation. With enough spankings, the disconnect can become permanent. If your child has disconnected from you, you are indeed the one who has been hurt.

When you discipline a child with physical aggression, you often initiate a power struggle. This activates resistance, reluctance, and resentment in the one who has received the discipline. Even if the child acquiesces, she often engages in revenge fantasies. That means she is wishing she could get you. If your spankings result in reluctance and resistance on the part of your child, once again it is you who has been hurt.

There is a name for a big person who hits little ones. That name is BULLY. If your child perceives you as a bully, you have lost again. You have lost stature in his or her eyes. You have injured your reputation in the heart and mind of your own child.

By jumping to the physical punishment stance you lose an opportunity to learn enlightened parenting skills. Not only does this strategy rarely teach the lesson you intend, it also deprives you of learning new verbal skills and parenting techniques that would add to your parenting toolbox. If the only tool you have is a hammer, you tend to look at everything as if it were a nail. Your effectiveness as a parent is hurt by relying on physical punishment and not developing additional skills.

Spanking a child meets the needs of the adult, not of the child. By satisfying your needs, you can quickly return to your own agenda. Sacrificed in the process is the family agenda, including the opportunity to debrief, listen, and seek consensus. If a sense of family is important to you, you undermine your goal by relying on the selfishness of spanking.

Spanking takes you in the opposite direction from becoming the parent you always wanted to be. Do you really feel like an effective parent when you spank your children? Does your image of yourself increase when you resort to hitting them? Do you say to yourself, "There, I've been a good parent again," when you lay your hand on your child's backside? If you have a grander vision of yourself as a parent than one who models "might makes right" to his children, then spanking hurts you.

Justifying in your mind that spanking children is necessary allows you to be unconscious about the work you need to do on your own anger issues. It stunts your growth as a mature parent and permits you to continue acting like a child who is attempting to raise children. Hitting children helps you stay little and does nothing to encourage you to move into adulthood.

Clearly, spanking has the potential to hurt your

children in many ways. There is no doubt about that. But don't delude yourself with the idea that it hurts them more than it hurts you. The hurt that occurs during spanking is not limited to one person. It hurts all involved. Why not stop hurting yourself and your children? Why not eliminate spanking from your parenting repertoire?

Check our blog site for Thomas Haller's informative blog on Spanking and the Bible, http://www.uncommon-parenting.com/2009/10/ spanking-be-gone/

So who is going to answer that question in the affirmative? Not any child we know.

Threatening a spanking does not build personal responsibility. At best, it induces forced compliance. It creates blind obedience that is directed from the outside. It does little to build self-discipline or self-responsibility. The child's inner authority is bypassed and he learns to rely on outer control from someone bigger and louder. What happens when the outer control leaves? Who controls the child now? How does a child function without an inner set of controls, ones he has not yet learned to trust?

"Jillian, if you don't stop talking back to me, you're going to sit in the time-out area until you learn to respect me!"

"You know that when children in this family won't put their toys away they have to sit in time-out. Is that what you want? If not, you'd better start putting those toys away right now."

"Rita, you're supposed to be in time-out. Get back in that chair and stay there quietly until your time is up. Now I have to reset the timer because you left the time-out chair early."

Parents across the country are using words such as these in an attempt to control a child's behavior with the increasingly popular discipline technique of "time-out."

Adults use time-outs with the best of intentions. They want a discipline technique that's an option to sarcasm, ridiculing, yelling, or shaming. They prefer not to spank or use other forms of physical punishment to control their children. So they opt for using a time-out. They know it's important to hold children accountable for their behaviors, and they use a time-out as a consequence of the choice the child has made.

These adults believe that placing a child in time-out will make him think about what he did wrong and learn not to do it anymore. They believe that the child will stop hitting in frustration after having enough opportunities to sit and think about hitting. They believe he will learn to pick up his toys, stop throwing sand, and start using kind words because he sat in his bedroom long enough to figure out why he was there.

As it is often practiced, a time-out is used for control. It is used as a threat. "If you don't stop that, you'll go to time-out." It is used to punish. "OK, that's it. You go to your room." When you use a time-out in these ways, you're teaching children that those with the power have the right to control others. You're showing them that might makes right and that the bigger gets to dominate the smaller.

Children being controlled by the threat of a time-out may indeed change their behavior. But when they do, the motivation to change is external.

The child hasn't been asked to think for herself or given the chance to internalize the need for a new behavior. Nor has she been taught any new behaviors. What she learns is to behave when the adult is near in fear of punishment. But she doesn't behave when the adult is not present because she hasn't learned to behave from the inside out. She is behaving only from the outside in.

When a time-out is used for punishment, it often creates resentment as children direct their anger and blame at the parents. They scheme about how to get even rather than contemplate alternatives to the behavior that got them the negative consequence. These feelings serve to disconnect them from the family rather than bring them closer.

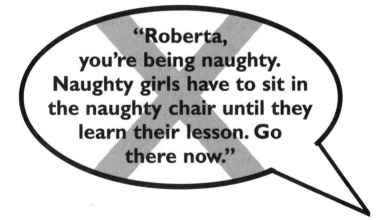

Many parents make it understood that their child is being sent to time-out because he or she has been naughty or bad. When you send a child to a specific area because he was "naughty" and make that clear to him, you send a message to the child that *he* is bad, that *he* is naughty. This use of time-out attacks the character of the child. It wounds the spirit and brands him as being *that way*. It results in feelings of low self-esteem and creates core beliefs of "I am wrong," "I am not worthy," and "I am naughty."

"Looks like you need a cool-down time. Let's take a time-out."

Time out as it was originally designed was an attempt to give children time to cool down. It was to provide a safe space and time for a child to calm herself. Creating time and space for a child to calm down so she can think is the first step toward creating an internal standard, an inner authority that guides the child's behavior. It is a move toward control from within rather than from the outside.

A healthy time-out is something one takes or is given when one needs a break from their surroundings. When an adult is overworked and feeling stress from their job, they take a time-out. It's called a vacation or a walk around the block.

When you're so angry that you can't think, you remove yourself from the situation and come back later when you can think clearly. That's a healthy time-out. When you come home from work exhausted and sit down on an easy chair for fifteen minutes, you're giving yourself a useful time-out.

A time-out period is what we need when we're sad and want to be alone. It's what we need when we're hurt and don't know what to say. A time-out is what we need when we're confused and don't know what to do. It is what we need when we're frustrated and don't know what we want. A time-out accesses an internal resting place where one goes to collect oneself, to reenergize and get ready to address the problem at hand.

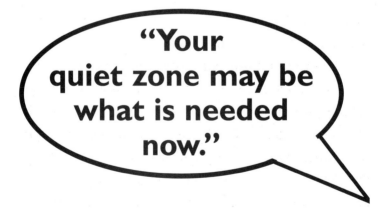

"Your quiet zone may be what is needed now."

Children also need time to calm their minds and relax their bodies when they're frustrated. They need a break from the world around them when they're yelling or angry. Children need an opportunity to get themselves ready to learn a new skill or face a problem. They need time to get back into a solution-seeking, problem-solving mode.

A time-out is not to be used as the punishment part of a discipline technique. It is the time a child needs to get into the right frame of mind so he or she can learn how to manage anger, curb aggression, or use a different set of words to express disappointment.

A child will only learn to manage his behavior when he is in the frame of mind that allows him to do that. Managing behavior, comparing possible outcomes, understanding consequences, choosing among options, and creating choices take place in the area of the brain called the frontal lobe. When your daughter is throwing a tantrum, she is not in her frontal lobe. Nor is your son using his frontal lobe when he's yelling, "I hate you."

When your child demonstrates physical behaviors such as hitting, kicking, biting, throwing objects, stomping feet, and swinging arms, she is in tantrum mode. Such behaviors are not generated in the cortex, where the frontal lobe is located. Yelling, screaming, crying, and other emotional behaviors are generated in the limbic brain, which assists in managing emotional content and is not typically a problem-solving area. It's important for parents, educators, and daycare providers to recognize these behaviors and understand that children are not in an appropriate mindset from which to engage in learning a new skill, solving a problem, or understanding the cause and effect relationship of the choices they have made.

To discipline a child in the middle of a tantrum or during an emotional outburst serves no useful purpose. The role of the adult at this time is to help the child pass through the tantrum or emotional phase and move into a behavior-management and problem-solving mode.

The appropriate use of a time-out is to provide the time and space a child needs to move into his frontal lobe and thus into a mode of thinking conducive to learning how to manage behavior.

The time-out is not the learning phase. It is not when teaching occurs. Taking time out is the getting-ready phase, the recollecting-one's-thoughts-and-feelings phase. A time-out is provided for a child to give her several minutes of solitude in a calming place, allowing the brain to slowly shift into higher cortical thinking and frontal lobe activation. When the child has made this transition, then and only then is the process of holding her accountable and teaching her how to do it differently next time appropriate.

"OK, you can take seven."

As practiced around the world today, the standard amount of time to be in time-out is correlated with the age of the child. For a seven-year-old, the rule suggests the child should sit in time-out for seven minutes. We disagree.

Some individuals move into the behavior-management and problem-solving mode of the brain faster than others do. For some children it could require only seconds, while for others it may take thirty minutes. Give your child whatever time he or she needs to get ready. That is the most effective use of a time-out.

Many parents allow children to return to the family group or resume their activity after they have stayed in time-out for a specific amount of time. A time-out used in this way becomes synonymous with "doing time." Once you've served your sentence, you're free to go about your business. "Doing time" does not work if raising responsible, caring, conscious children is your goal.

"**Looks like you're calm and ready to talk.**"

If a time-out is indeed used as a gift of time and space, it is the time *after* having taken time out that becomes the most important. This is when you follow up by teaching a needed lesson, debriefing the previous scenario, and creating plans for next time. Use the time after a time-out to debrief and help your children learn to manage their behavior through the guidance and instruction you give them. This will help them develop a better understanding of the consequences of their behavior. They will be more receptive to suggestions on how to correct their behavior. They will feel more empowered and more confident in being able to manage their behavior in the future. They will be more likely to see themselves as capable, responsible people.

If you want your child to see himself as a responsible and successful person, to learn to get along with the family, to build positive relationships with others, and to increase feelings of connected-ness with you, stop using time-outs as a punish-ment. Use them as a positive interruption of an undesirable behavior so the child can calm himself and be receptive to the guidance, instruction, and lessons in accountability that follow.

"In this family you have the opportunity to be with your friends," Mr. Wilson explained to his eleven-year-old daughter. "Your responsibility is to be home on time. Like a lot of things in this family, opportunity equals responsibility, or responsibility equals opportunity. If the responsibility stays strong, so does the opportunity. If the responsibility falls off, the opportunity will drop accordingly."

Shannon Wilson understood exactly what her father meant. She had heard that equation many times previously. If she chose to come home on time, there would be further opportunities to be with her friends. If she chose to come home late, she would be choosing to have fewer opportunities to demonstrate her responsibility.

Shannon knew her father wasn't kidding, because the Dynamic Discipline Equation *opportunity equals responsibility* had been in effect in her home for many years. Indeed, it was the cornerstone of the Wilson's effort to have their children grow increasingly toward becoming self-responsible adults.

For more on the Dynamic Discipline Equation, see our book *The Only Three Discipline Strategies You Will Ever Need,* www.personalpowerpress.com.

Choose, Decide, Pick

"If you <u>choose</u> to throw your dolls, you will be <u>deciding</u> to have them on the shelf until after lunch."

"If you <u>choose</u> to earn anything less than a C this semester, you will be <u>deciding</u> to have a tutor on Saturday mornings until the grade is improved."

"When you <u>decide</u> to spend your allowance the first day you get it, you are <u>choosing</u> to have no money for the remainder of the week."

"When you <u>pick</u> which show to watch, you are <u>choosing</u> to pass on the others."

Choose, decide, and *pick* are linking words that will help you add meaning and strength to the Dynamic Discipline Equation. They help children perceive the connection between cause and effect. They will allow your children to see that if they choose *this* they can create *that.* This style of Parent Talk puts the child in control of the outcomes he creates in his life. It allows him to become decisive, empowered, and increasingly responsible.

"If my kid doesn't put gas in the car, she's not getting it for a month," a father once told us at a workshop. Thomas told him politely, "Sir, with all due respect, you can't learn to put gas in the car if you don't have it."

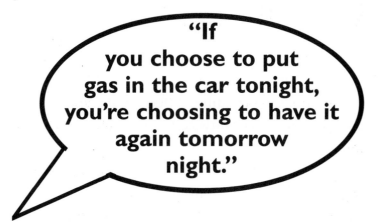

"If you choose to put gas in the car tonight, you're choosing to have it again tomorrow night."

Please know that a consequence need not be severe to be effective. It is not the severity of a consequence that has the impact. It is the certainty. It is the certainty that specific, logical consequences follow actions that allows children to trust the discipline process.

What is certain in this case is that this teenager is not getting the car tomorrow night if she chooses not to put gas in it. It is useful to start over the next weekend so she gets another opportunity to be responsible.

It is your consistency in implementing consequences that holds a discipline strategy together. If consequences are implemented with regularity, children learn over time that if they *choose* to leave their bike in the middle of the driveway, they have *decided* to have it hung up in the garage for a few days. Teenagers come to know that if they *choose* to visit off-limit sites on the computer, they have *chosen* to lose computer privileges for a few days.

When the consequence occurs consistently, children can count on that fact and plan accordingly. They see themselves as responsible for the outcomes they are creating. Effective discipline that promotes responsibility calls for parents to structure consequences in a way that puts the child in control and allows him to feel responsible for the outcomes that result from his actions.

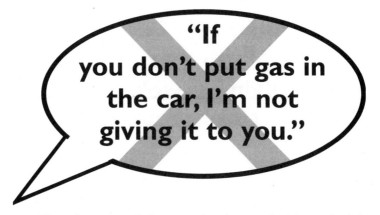

The absence of the words *choose, decide* and *pick* in this verbalization removes the power and control from the child and places it in the hands of the parent. The child becomes angry at the parent if she isn't given the car because she perceives the adult as the one who is responsible for the outcome she herself produced with her choice to not put gas in the vehicle. She is less likely to look inward and hold herself responsible.

"If you don't stop complaining, we're not going to the movies."

Consequences are not to be used to control, manipulate, demonstrate power, or get even. Attempting to use consequences for control crosses the line and becomes punishment.

Punishment, using force unrelated to the behavior, comes across as retribution. Disciplining with punishment places the child in a position of being "done to" by others in a position of authority. The child, now feeling powerless, does not see himself as being in control of the outcome. He sees himself as the victim.

When children perceive that they're in control of whether or not they experience consequences or outcomes, they are empowered. They learn to see themselves as the cause of what happens to them. They realize that they personally create the results that show up in their lives by the choices they make. For discipline to be effective, it's necessary for children to feel they have power and control.

> **"If you don't pick up your toys, you get no dessert during dinner tonight."**

This is an example of a parent picking a consequence that is unrelated to the behavior. What do toys on the floor have to do with dessert? Nothing.

If a consequence is unrelated to the behavior, it's interpreted in the child's mind as punishment. The child's attention then moves from her choice of the behavior to the person applying the punishment. She is now looking outside of herself rather than within. She is focusing on what is being "done" to her instead of what on what she could learn from her choice and doing something different next time.

Your use of the words *choose, decide,* and *pick* does not make up for choosing an unrelated consequence. "If you choose to leave your toys on the floor, you have decided to have no dessert tonight" doesn't change the fact that toys on the floor have nothing to do with dessert.

"If you choose to leave your toys on the floor, you are choosing to have me pick them up and put them in a box for a week. You can decide." This is an example of a consequence that is directly related to the choice made by the child. If this child leaves toys on the floor, something happens to the toys. Dessert isn't even mentioned.

Some examples of structuring a consequence more directly related to the behavorial choice made by the child include:

"If you choose to drink all the Pepsi this weekend, you have decided to go without it the rest of the week."

"If you decide to put your dirty clothes in the clothes hamper, you will have chosen to have them cleaned by Monday."

"If you choose to throw these toys, you will have decided to have them on the shelf for awhile."

This style of Parent Talk focuses on the negative. Strengthen your communication of consequences by speaking from a positive position. "If you choose to clean up your room, you have decided to invite a guest over." State what will happen if, rather than what *won't* happen if.

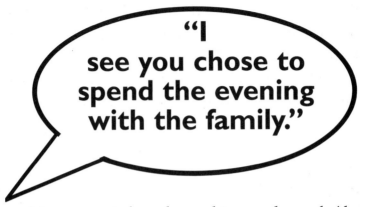

"**I see you chose to spend the evening with the family.**"

Many parents have learned to use *choose, decide,* and *pick* when communicating consequences. They have also learned how to keep the consequence related to the behavior and state it in positive terms. Their challenge comes not in learning to use effective verbal skills but rather in developing the will to follow through. For many parents it's easier to cave in and let the child off the hook than to follow through with the consequences.

Please do not bail kids out. Do not rescue. Do not save. Please allow them to experience the legitimate consequences of their actions. Unless you enforce consequences regularly, your children will not appreciate the relationship between cause and effect. They will not perceive that the choices they make produce results. Do you want your children to come to believe: *My choices created this; therefore, if I make different choices, I could create something else?* If so, implement the consequences consistently. That will produce your best chance of motivating your children to make responsible decisions from within.

Bring us to your school or church to make a parent presentation and you will hear us say, "Holding children accountable for their actions is one of the most loving things you can do as a parent." And we mean that.

"That's a healthy limit.

Do you have family rules? Are you getting some resistance to those rules? Are you being constantly asked to explain why a certain rule exists? Maybe it's time to end family rules and begin having healthy limits.

Being home by nine o'clock is not a family rule. It is a healthy limit. Having one piece of candy per day, watching one hour of TV per day, and going to bed by eight o'clock are not rules. They are healthy limits.

It's easier for children to argue against rules than against healthy limits. Healthy limits are easier for you to defend. "My main job as a parent is to keep you safe and healthy. That's why we have healthy limits."

Wearing your seat belt is a healthy limit. Using the car seat is a healthy limit. Not smoking is a healthy limit. Using words instead of fists is a healthy limit. Putting yourself in a quiet area when you're upset is a healthy limit.

Think of it this way. Would you rather be a parent who creates and enforces rules or one who sets healthy limits?

Anger is not helpful in a discipline situation. When you discipline in anger, the child's attention focuses on your strong emotion. He looks outward to the person applying the punishment rather than inward to his own internal reaction to the results of the choice he made.

When holding a child accountable for his choices, sincere empathy is much more effective than anger. "Bummer, what a shame. I bet that will be a challenge for you now" is empathy that maintains a positive connection between you and the child even as you hold him accountable for his actions. When the child hears empathy instead of anger, he is more likely to look inside and to notice the connection between cause (his choice) and effect (the consequence).

Making children wrong for their behavior is counterproductive to raising them to be responsible adults. An effective discipline system does not make children right or wrong for their behavior. It simply holds them accountable for it.

If your child fails to put her bike in the garage as agreed, don't make her wrong. Don't make her lazy. Don't make her forgetful. Don't make her irresponsible. Just make her someone who doesn't get to ride her bike for three days—the consequence you agreed on earlier.

Even if the problem reoccurs over time, refrain from making your child wrong. Blaming and fault-finding don't help children learn how to make different choices and behave differently in the future. Fixing the problem is more important than fixing blame. Join with your children in the search for solutions and model for them that you value solving problems more than you do assigning blame and handing out punishments.

"You're grounded until you can learn to talk with respect."

When we choose to use consequences, the aim isn't to make our children comply. The goal is to present choices, allow them to choose, and give them room to learn from the results of those choices. With the consequence system, children learn a lesson from either the positive or negative outcome they create.

A child's compliance or noncompliance has nothing to do with the effectiveness of a discipline system. When discipline strategies demand compliance, as when the parent keeps increasing the severity of the punishment until the child complies, children learn that adults have power and they don't.

Punishing children with increasing severity until they pick up their toys might get them to pick up their toys. It will not teach them to take responsibility for their toys or create internal motivation to produce the desired behavior.

With consequences, we present a choice. "You can choose to pick up your toys or you can choose to leave them here. If you choose to pick them up, you will have decided to use them for the next week. If you decide to leave them here, I will pick them up, and you will have decided not to have them available for a week. You decide." With this style of discipline, the child may choose to pick up his toys or he may choose to leave them. Either way, it's perfect. If he picks them up, it's perfect. You don't have to do it. If he leaves them there, it's perfect. It's the perfect time to help him learn what happens when he chooses not to pick up his toys.

"OK, I'll bail you out this time."

Do you bail out your children? If so, you are inadvertently teaching them they do not have to act responsibly because they won't be held accountable for their choices.

If you're running lunch, homework, gym shoes, band instruments, or other forgotten objects to school, you are bailing out your children. You are not giving them a real reason to remember the forgotten object next time. Your job is to teach your children a system for remembering. Their job is to use the system.

Do you return home to get forgotten shin guards for soccer or a teeth guard for karate? Again, teach your children a system for remembering. If they forget, allow them to experience the natural outcome of their behavior. Give them a real-life reason to remember in the future. Why would they ever have to remember if someone keeps bailing them out?

Do you give advances on allowances? If so, you are rescuing. One of the reasons for giving allowances is to help children learn that if they spend it all the first day, there is no more until next week. You are depriving children of the opportunity to learn an important lesson when you bail them out. Allow them to deal with the outcomes of their spending, saving, or budgeting choices.

Are you a rescuer with your children's homework? Do you care more than they do? To step out of the rescuer role, be available to help with homework, set a study time, and create a study place. Once again, your job is to create the structure. Their job is to use it. If they come to you at nine p.m. and inform you they need a poster board for a project, resist the urge to jump in the car and drive all over town trying to find one. As the saying goes, procrastination on their part does not necessitate an emergency on your part. Allow them to experience the consequences.

Stop reminding children. Instead, give them a responsibility. Allow them to choose or choose not to do it and implement the consequences with love in your heart. If you continue to remind your children, you are becoming a crutch that increases their impotence. You are teaching them that they don't have to remember their responsibilities because the *reminder person* will remind them. You have enough responsibilities as a parent. Being the reminder person is not one of them. Give it up by giving that responsibility back to your children.

"You should have told her . . ."

"My advice is . . ."

"You should call her right now and apologize."

We often tell children they should do this or that. We give them our sage advice whether they want it or not. This does nothing to help them learn to think for themselves. It does not promote responsibility nor help them see themselves as capable.

One helpful Parent Talk alternative to "You should have . . . " is "I wonder . . . ."

Instead of saying, "You should have told her," say, "I wonder what would have happened if you had told her."

Replace "You shouldn't have said that" with "I wonder how he would have reacted if you had said it this way."

"I wonder what you have learned from this" is more effective than "I hope you learned a lesson here."

"I wonder if these words would have sounded kinder."

"I wonder what choice you will make next

time."

We wonder if you will use "I wonder" with your children to invite them to do their own thinking.

"I KNOW YOU CAN'T SPEND MONEY YOU DON'T HAVE. THAT'S WHY I WANT YOU TO GIVE ME SOME."

When your child comes to you with a concern, most likely you can solve the problem. As an experienced adult, you have the answers. You know what to do. Come up with the solution often, and your child begins to see you as the problem solver, the fixer, the rescuer. Your child loses confidence in his or her own ability to handle problems and fails to build skills to use when you are not around.

Using discipline strategies that build self-responsibility and personal power in children requires believing that fixing the problem is more important than fixing blame. Searching for solutions puts you in a teaching mode. Handing out punishments casts you in the role of policeperson, judge, and warden. Personal responsibility increases when errors are corrected, not when they are punished. Energy spent blaming your son for spilling milk does not improve his milk-pouring skills for next time. Angrily reprimanding your daughter for forgetting to feed the dog doesn't ensure that she will feed the dog tomorrow.

When you invest your time searching for and creating solutions with your children, problems do not need to be continually addressed. By solving a parenting problem while refraining from punishing, you empower your children.

Instead of giving answers, consider asking questions.

Questions can help your child consider options: "What have you thought of so far?" "What other possibilities do you see?"

Questions can help your child focus and clarify

goals: "What are you attempting to accomplish here?" "How would you like it to turn out?"

You communicate trust when you ask your child questions: "What can you do to create it the way you want it?" "How would you handle this if no one were around to ask?"

Questions allow you to become the facilitator. They help you step out of the rescuing role: "What do you think would happen if you did that?" "How would that feel if it were happening to you?" "So what do you think you will do?"

If your goal is raising a responsible, confident, skill-oriented solution seeker, ask questions that require thinking instead of offering solutions.

The Niemis have a magic carpet in their home. To the untrained eye it appears to be a small oval rug that sits in front of the fireplace. It serves as a safety net should burning embers make it through the fireplace screen and fall onto the floor. The protective nature of this rug is an important and appreciated function, but it is not related in any way to its magical attributes. Their magic rug plays a more important role. It produces magical and elegant solutions to family conflicts. This is how it works.

Last week Jean Paul began an algebra unit in his fifth-grade math class. His older sister, Juliette, had been studying algebra throughout her eighth-grade school year. When Jean Paul made an error on one homework problem, Juliette leaped to the rescue. Envisioning herself as a future math teacher, she saw this opportunity as a chance to practice her future trade. There was a slight problem, however. Jean Paul did not want to be the practice dummy. A light disagreement began, gradually escalated its way into bickering, and then bloomed into a full-blown argument complete with angry tones and loud voices.

When loud turned to louder, Mr. Niemi stepped in. "Sounds like you two are in need of the magic carpet," he suggested. Both children knew what that meant. The magic carpet had been used many times in their home.

Each child sat on one end of the carpet facing the other. They had learned over time that when people in their family sit face to face on the magic carpet and talk about their conflict, magic solutions appear. Sometimes the solutions come quickly. At other times it takes a while for a solution to surface, but no one has ever seen it fail.

Will the magic carpet help these two children

create a magic solution to the algebra problem dilemma? It will if they keep talking until they find a solution to which both can agree.

"Let me know when you find an elegant solution," Mr. Niemi remarked. "I want to hear how this carpet works its magic in this case." Amid his children's grumbling, he returned to his computer and began to work.

The father listened in as their conversation began. It didn't take long before he realized he was the only one listening. Both children were talking at the same time. Frustration mounted, voice volume increased, and emotion was vented.

He reentered the scene. "I don't hear any magic yet," he observed. "He won't listen to me," Juliette complained. "She won't listen to me," replied Jean Paul. It was clearly time to give the magic carpet some assistance.

Rummaging through the kitchen, this parent found a large wooden spoon. Returning to the children, he told them, "This is a talking stick." It was the closest thing he could find to a stick at the moment. "Native Americans used talking sticks during council meetings," he explained. "The rules are simple. You can only talk if you are holding the stick (spoon). When you're finished talking, pass the stick to the other person and don't talk until it is handed back to you. Understand?"

"Yep," both children replied.

He then handed the stick to Juliette and sat back to listen to the conversation. Although the children followed the talking-stick rules, it was a good ten minutes before any real listening took place. Both were intent on telling their side of the story and proving how right they were. Eventually, Juliette and Jean Paul remembered that in order to get off the rug they were going to have to find a solution that both could live with.

A solution was offered. It was rejected and another was proposed in its place. From their spots on the rug, reasons, rationale, and counterproposals were suggested by one child or the other. Clearly, the oval carpet was working its magic.

Twenty minutes into the magic carpet session a solution was offered and accepted. Juliette would listen to Jean Paul explain how he did the equation. Jean Paul would then listen to Juliette explain her understanding of the math problem the way her teacher taught it in eighth grade. Conflict was resolved and consensus reached. The siblings were now at peace, implementing the agreed-upon solution.

It isn't easy being a parent who helps children grow in responsibility by learning to solve their own problems. It sure helps to have a magic carpet.

"But I deserve a new pair of jeans."

"I don't know why you won't let me go over to Arturo's."

"I'm old enough to handle that."

Each of these children wanted a concession on the part of the parent. Their statements are among those often delivered to parents by their children. To each request, the conscious parent responded, "Convince me."

"Convince me" is Parent Talk that puts the burden back on the child. This phrase tells the child that it is not the parent who is responsible for coming up with reasons why the child is prevented from doing a certain thing. It is the child who must come up with reasons why the parent should reconsider. It is no longer the parent who has to do the convincing. That responsibility has been shifted to the child, where it belongs.

Hearing "Convince me," the child is required to do the thinking. The parent is freed up from thinking for the child. "Convince me" helps children learn how to construct a reasonable argument. This is a valuable skill they can use throughout their lives with peers or other adults.

If you hear yourself about to say, "Because I said so, that's why," stop. Respond instead with "Convince me." Listen and learn as your child begins to think for herself.

"You're a bully."
"You are definitely a troublemaker."
"You're a whiner."
"You're such a slob."

Be careful about attaching labels to your children's behaviors. Know that your labels will affect how they behave. The words you use to describe them create or strengthen the way they view themselves. How they view themselves determines what they come to believe about themselves. What they believe about themselves influences how they behave in the future.

Children are not their behavior. They are not their report card. They are not their table manners. They are not their anger. Those behaviors are only their behaviors in this present moment. It is not who and what they are as human beings. They are a child of God.

Learn to use language that separates the deed from the doer. "I like you and I don't like that behavior" are the words to use and the attitude to take to separate the deed from the doer. It tells the child that it's the behavior that is inappropriate. Love remains for the child while the individual behavior is not appreciated.

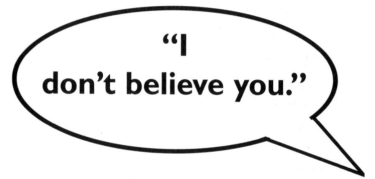

To reduce power struggles over lying, say, "I don't believe you," instead of "You're lying." This Parent Talk phrase tells the child about you and what you think. When you accuse children of lying, it's easy for them to argue that they were telling the truth; however, they cannot argue about what you believe.

"I don't believe you" is about you and your beliefs. "You're lying" is about them and invites defensiveness. Let your Parent Talk speak about you when you confront lying and you will incur less resistance and resentment.

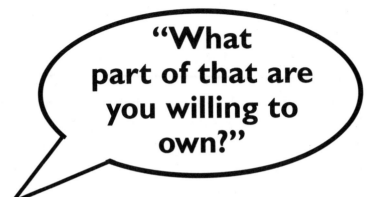

"**What part of that are you willing to own?**"

"He made me do it."

"It was his fault we got there late."

"He started it."

"She gave me a D."

"He got me in trouble."

"She steered me wrong."

"Time just got away from me."

"I didn't have time."

Children often use language that denies responsibility for their actions, feelings, and choices. This way of speaking robs them of their personal power by assigning the responsibility for their behaviors to someone or something else. When you see others as responsible for your responses to life, you give your power away by disowning your personal responsibility.

You can fall down repeatedly and you won't be unempowered until you say someone pushed you. We need to teach children to own their reactions to life situations and to discover where they indeed did have power.

When your child says, "He started it," respond with, "What part of that fracas are you willing to own?" If he suggests, "I didn't have time," ask, "What choices did you make that contributed to being late?" "What did you do to help create the D?" is a helpful response to "She gave me a D" if responsibility is your goal.

Listen to your children's language patterns this week. Then monitor your own way of speaking. If your children are using self-responsible language, what part of that phenomenon are you willing to own?

RELATIONSHIPS

An important part of successfully raising responsible, caring, conscious children lies in helping them create positive, mutually satisfying relationships in their lives. You want to have a warm and satisfying relationship with your children yourself. You want all your children to get along well with each other and treat one another with love and respect. You want your children to value the extended family and feel genuine affection for grandparents, aunts and uncles, cousins and other relatives.

At school you'd probably like teachers to write the following remarks on your child's report card.

"He gets along well with everyone."

"She has lots of friends."

"He makes friends easily."

"She is a pleasure to work with."

Wouldn't it be nice if your daughter's soccer coach said, "Her teammates voted her as captain because she's so friendly and helps everyone"?

We bet you'd like your children to bring home friends who are positive, polite, trustworthy, cooperative, and honest. You'd like your son to date a young woman who is respectful of others and expects others to be the same with her. You want your children to choose a spouse who knows how to communicate and settle disagreements in positive ways, stays connected, and works continually to build a meaningful relationship with your adult son or daughter.

Coworkers, bosses, and employees will play an important role in your children's lives. Will your son or daughter be able to network in ways that create mutual success? Will they be able to interface meaningfully with the head of the accounting department and with the advertising committee? Much of success in a person's professional life is dependent on gaining cooperation and productivity from other people. All of that requires relationships that work.

So how do you teach your children about the importance of relationships and how to create them? When, where, and how do you deliver those lessons?

You can begin today. The Parent Talk that follows will help you enhance your child's relationships with friends, relatives, and, most importantly, with you. If you haven't already done it, start today to help your child create lasting and quality relationships by implementing the ideas which resonate for you.

"I don't want you going over to his house again."

"You'll have to find different friends."

"She's not a good friend to have."

The statements above are examples of Parent Talk designed to control the child's friends. They reflect the parents' desire that their children choose friends wisely because the parents' belief system includes mental concepts such as: You are who you hang around with; You can expect to earn no more money than the average of your six best friends; Other people will judge you by your friends. The parents may also fear that some close friends might be a negative influence on their child. Therefore, they make statements like, "You can't associate with him in the future."

While this degree of control over your child's friends may be possible up to the age of eight or nine, the ability to exercise that control stops there. That's right. Around fourth grade you lose the power to choose your child's friends. Why? You can't control who they see because you are not continuously in their presence for the entire day. Your children ride a bus, go to school, hang out in the neighborhood, and play on a soccer team. Therefore, you lose your power to enforce the command, "You can't see him anymore." Since you can't enforce that command, you're wasting your breath to issue it.

While you lose your ability to *control* your child's choice of friends at this point in their lives, you do not lose your ability to *influence* who they choose as friends. If you accept the fact that your child is choosing her own friends, which she actually is, and assume that posture as you talk with her, you can still have a positive impact on her thinking and her choices by using well chosen and well constructed Parent Talk.

"William always helps pick up the messes you guys make."

"I noticed Ahmed doesn't gossip about your other friends when they're not here."

"Rebecca made sure everyone got a turn with her new game."

This type of Parent Talk points your child to positive character traits in his friends. Comments like those above help him to recognize and appreciate the fact that you see some of his friends' positive traits.

"Tell me what you like about Clarissa."

"What strengths do you see in Lynda?" and "Tell me what you enjoy about Robert" are examples of Parent Talk that will help you understand the positives *your child* sees in her friends. Use a loving and interested tone as you pose these questions. If you fail to comprehend the strengths *she* sees in her friends, she will be less likely to take a serious look at the character traits *you* see.

"I hope some of your gentle ways will rub off on him."

"Maybe your positive attitude can influence how he looks at the world" and "Being polite is a nice way to help your friend Bonnie learn interper-

"EDDIE AND I ARE GOING TO BE BEST FRIENDS AS SOON AS WE GET ALL THE KINKS WORKED OUT."

sonal skills" are comments that reinforce the strengths you see in your own child and a way to gently invite him to look at what you have noticed about his friends. This kind of Parent Talk is designed to get your child to think. It does not instruct him what to do about his friends.

Other Parent Talk phrases that invite your child to do the thinking include:

"I wonder if Marie makes fun of *you* when *you're* not present."

"I'd be a bit worried about feeling pressured to drink if I was with her."

"Do you ever worry that people might think you feel the same way that Sean does about Jews (blacks, Hispanics, Italians, women, Muslims, Christians)?"

"Is it difficult for you to stick up for your other friends when he starts to harass them?"

"Why do you think there is a difference between your study habits and his?"

Advice your children have not asked for will fall on deaf ears. Orders will hit a brick wall. Nonjudgmental information has a reasonable chance to get through to them and help them think through an issue. Offer information on their friends free of judgment, ridicule, or sarcasm and you may develop the influence you desire.

"Let
me give you a hug."

Your children's current and future relationship
with others (friends and siblings) begins with their
relationship with you. You teach them how to relate
to others best by how you relate to them now. Your
relationship with your child is his or her first and
most important model of what an effective relationship looks, feels, and sounds like.

From day one, a positive relationship includes
huge doses of appropriate touch. Bond with your
children with an abundance of touch. Yes, teenagers
too. Cuddle, massage, stroke, hold, walk hand in
hand, hug, and connect physically. Show affection,
concern, and caring with a pat on the back, a high
five, or a light squeeze on the shoulder.

Also touch with your eyes. Eyes have been
described as "the windows of the soul." Eyes can
communicate "I care about you" or "I don't care."
Eyes send the message "You are important to me"
or "Right now something else is more important to
me than you are."

You cannot spoil your baby by handling her too much. Babies need to be touched, squeezed, coddled, and held. Babies cry because they are hungry, sick, wet, messy, or desire attention. Pick up your baby and hold her. Do it as often as you like. You cannot spoil a baby.

One of the main jobs of a parent is to help all family members understand and feel that a family is a safe place where everyone can feel connected, loved, appreciated, and secure. This is where a child learns to be an integral part of something larger than himself. This is where he discovers that we can count on each other, trust each other, and give and get from one another. Here is where he first develops an understanding of the concept of us/we/our rather than I/me/my.

Yes, independence is important to children of all ages. And so too are the feelings of belonging and interdependence. Once children have experienced the security of living in a loving family, they are better equipped to accept the challenges inherent in becoming more independent.

In a loving, supportive family one's latest hairstyle is not the subject of ridicule. Neither is the latest social blunder or public mistake. A major function of a family is to create a supporting atmosphere free from shame, ridicule, and teasing.

"But I was only teasing," a workshop participant once told us. "We do it all the time," she added. "We all think it's funny. They all like it."

No, it is not funny. And they do not all like it. Thinly veiled sarcasm and teasing is a putdown. It has no place in a loving family where you are modeling effective, supportive, nurturing, affirming, respectful relationships.

Sara spent an hour one Saturday afternoon tossing a small beach ball at a plastic basketball hoop her father had brought home from a garage sale. Her first efforts missed the hoop by several feet. None of them hit the backboard. Her father stood by, retrieving each shot and returning the ball to her for another attempt. He also made descriptive comments after each shot. His Parent Talk was deliberate and focused. He gave supportive comments that were limited to describing what happened.

"You got close to the backboard."

"You almost hit it that time."

"Wow, only a foot away."

"You got it on the rim."

"Wow, a two-bouncer. It hit the rim twice."

When the ninth attempt went through the hoop, he exclaimed, "You did it! You got it in." Sara immediately ran to find her mother. "Mommy, Mommy, I did it. I got it in the hole!" she informed her mother. "You sound so excited. That must have been fun," her mother replied.

Notice that evaluative praise was not present in the Parent Talk of either of Sara's parents. No one said "Good job," "Excellent," or "Wonderful." By keeping evaluative praise out of their verbal responses, they left room for the child to draw the conclusion. They allowed their child to make the evaluation. One important function of families is that of support and encouragement without judging, evaluating, rating and ranking the efforts of one another.

"How shall we spend the money in the charity jar?"

"How shall we celebrate New Year's Eve?"

"What are we going to make Grandpa for his birthday?"

Shared decision-making brings people together and helps them feel connected. Having input, being listened to, listening to others' input, and reaching consensus is glue that bonds a family together. Every family member from youngest to oldest gets to have a say and feel that their ideas and opinions have value.

Parent Talk that values the opinions of others includes:

"Say some more."

"What is your opinion?"

"How do you feel about this, Chantel?"

"I'm not sure we're all listening to Larkin. Let's make sure he gets his turn, too."

"What other possibilities are there for solving this?"

"Wait a minute. We are not judging ideas right now. We're just collecting them."

Not sure what to discuss at a family meeting? Maybe it's time to convene one and ask others for their ideas on what to talk about. The process is more important that the product.

Building family solidarity is covered in depth in the chapter "The Tenth Commitment" in *The 10 Commitments: Parenting with Purpose,* www.person-alpowerpress.com.

"Where shall we go on vacation this year?"

Why not pick a destination together by establishing a mutual plan? Allow every member in the family to have input on the type of vacation and/or activities he or she would like to experience. Reach consensus on what type of vacation you want to create. Then brainstorm all the possible sites to visit and potential activities. Build a list of things you want to do, making sure that each family member has at least one of their top priorities on the list.

By allowing everyone to have a say, you build commitment and lower resistance toward activities that may be of less interest. By allowing every family member to have input, ownership is established. Each person can now look forward to the specific part of the vacation he or she has chosen while allowing other family members to enjoy different aspects of the vacation.

If your children are younger, establish the destination with your spouse and present the various options to the children for discussion. As they become older, increase their input on decisions. That the discussion happens is more important than the specific conclusions reached.

"It's time to debrief."

Debriefing is an opportunity for family members, both children and adults, to take a look at their behaviors and learn from them. It is the missing link in most parenting being done today.

Regardless of the subject or intended lesson, you don't learn from your experience. You learn from debriefing your experience. Yes, you can learn by being told how to play goal in soccer. You can learn more about it by actually having the experience of playing goal for a game or two. But the real learning will take place if someone invests the time to help you debrief it.

When you debrief, you reflect on your experience, think about it, talk about it, and come to some conclusions about it. Debriefing helps bring your behaviors to consciousness. You take a look at how you behaved. You compare that to how you wish you had behaved. This process helps you think critically and develop an internal standard. Debriefing is a time to make plans for improvement and set goals for next time. It is also a time to celebrate successes.

Debriefing is essential to effective parenting if you want your children to integrate positive behaviors into their lives.

"On the whole . . ." is the beginning of a debriefing question that asks children to think. It is asking them to make a generalization about their vacation.

When your vacation, party, weekend, trip to Grandma's, journey to the zoo, or rainy-day Saturday is over, invest a few minutes in debriefing. You can do this at the kitchen table, spread out on the front lawn, or in the hot tub. It matters less where you are and more that you initiate and lead this type of dialogue.

Parent Talk that debriefs and asks children to think includes:

"What did you *hear* this week that would indicate we were having fun?"

"What are some ways we can remember to show Grandma more respect in the future?"

"What was your favorite part and why?"

"What procedures did we follow to make sure that everyone had a good time?"

"If you rated this trip on a scale of one to ten, what number would you give it? Why?"

"What do we want to remember to bring next time?"

"How could we have improved our experience of this day?"

"What options exist for our next trip?"

"How well do you think we handled disagreements?"

"Sum up what happened at the zoo that prevented or allowed you to have fun."

"How well did you do with Grandma's impatience compared to how well you did last time?"

"How would you rate our family's responsibility with the environment at the lake this trip?"

"What goals shall we set for next time in terms of clean-up?"

It is not necessary to ask this many questions to have a highly effective debriefing session. Four or five questions, mixed with real listening and interest, will suffice.

**"HELLO, MRS. HORTON? COULD YOU
STOP BY SCHOOL TODAY?"**

The age of the electronic parent is upon us. There can be no question about that. It only takes a brief walk through a local department store or mall to notice that the preferred gift for most children older than the age of three is electronic. Parents are buying computer games, iPods, TVs, videos, and cell phones at an ever-increasing rate. In addition, they now purchase electronic "toys" that they believe help their children learn to say words, count, write letters, and even read.

Make no mistake about this–electronic purchases are changing the face of parenting. The role of parenting is being turned over to the electronic world, and this does not always benefit the child or the parent. Let's take a closer look.

It's not new or even surprising information that children in the United States now spend, on average, six and one-half hours a day exposed to electronic media that includes TV, computers, listening to music, and playing video games. What is surprising is that so few parents seem to care or are willing to do anything about it.

Consider that young children are now regularly hearing an electronic voice pronounce words to them instead of hearing their parent's voice reading aloud. Preschoolers and kindergartners are getting a jump-start into color identification and letter writing with computer programs instead of drawing and coloring with Mom or Dad at the kitchen table. School-age children are occupied for hours with handheld video games instead of an engrossing paperback book. Adolescents and teens are listening to hours of music on iPods instead of communicating with the family. There is no time to debrief because everyone in the family is plugged into some electronic device.

Does it occur to you that something is missing here? It's called connectedness and family interaction. The expanding use of electronic media as a substitute for involved parenting has created the Great Family Disconnect. Increased emphasis on TV, the Internet, and video games is creating an emotional gap between parent and child and severely limiting family interaction. The electronic takeover of parental responsibility is creating family distance, isolation, and a decrease in feelings of belonging and connectedness.

Disconnecting from family is currently growing in direct proportion to the strength of connection our children feel to their favorite electronic device.

Simply put, electronic media in a child's life increases isolation.

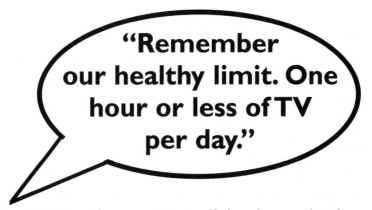

"Remember our healthy limit. One hour or less of TV per day."

It is time for parents to pull the plug on the electronic takeover and put the human touch back into the parenting equation. It is time for parents to realize that six and one-half hours a day of being plugged into media leaves children little time to plug into their family. It is time for parents to recognize that there is no healthy reason for a child to carry a video game with him wherever he goes, or for a parent to make a child's bedroom so attractive and so media friendly that she wants to spend most of her time there by herself. It is time for parents to accept their parenting responsibilities and make a commitment to active, "hands-on," parenting.

While riding in the car, unplug the headphones, turn off the DVD player, and tell your children a story about the day they were born or about a mouse that lives under the deck. Shut down the computer, turn off the Xbox, and play a game of chess, checkers, or Monopoly together. Stand up, walk away from the TV, and go shoot baskets, skip rope, or ride bikes with your child. Build a snowman or go on a nature walk. Invest time in your children rather than in the newest electronic device.

Don't wait until your parenting power pack goes dead. Make a commitment today to be the best parent you can be by being present and interactive in your child's life on a regular basis. Take back the sacred role of parenting children from the electronic world. Be the parent you are being called to be.

"Stop crying."

"Don't worry about it. You can get another one."

"So what do you want me to do about it?"

"Why don't you just suck it up?"

"Pouting isn't going to get you anywhere."

The statements above and others similar to them are often uttered by parents whose homes suffer from Empathy Deficit Disorder. Empathy Deficit Disorder, or EDD, as it is sometimes called, is a chronic condition brought on by parents' refusal to acknowledge a child's feelings or by their efforts to diminish those feelings when they are expressed. This condition in children is an offshoot of parental hurry-up sickness engaged in by adults who don't take time to listen or respond to a child's feelings because getting on with the business of the day is more important than investing the time to make empathetic responses to the people they love.

The long-term existence of EDD results in a lack of closeness between parents and children and produces a severe disconnect that can take years to repair. Children are often left bewildered by their parents' apparent lack of caring and concern for their feelings. In turn, they learn to numb their own feelings as a coping mechanism to protect themselves from experiencing the hurt and emptiness they feel but cannot describe or totally understand at a young age.

Sadly, negative messages learned about empathy and caring are often adopted by children in their relationships with their siblings and with others outside the home.

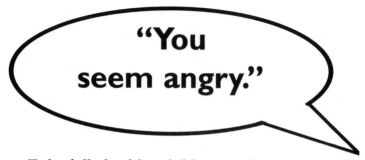

"You seem angry."

To be fully healthy, children need parents, teachers, and other adults to respond to their feelings in positive ways. This includes using feeling words when children are caught up in strong emotion (sadness or joy, anger or love, fear or faith).

"You look like you're frustrated."

"You seem sad."

"You sound like you're bubbling over with happiness."

This kind of Parent Talk communicates to children that their feelings are normal and part of being a fully functioning human being. In addition, using validating language puts Empathy Deficit Disorder on the run by giving love, nurturing, and comfort when your children are upset. Take your child onto your lap and hug him if he fell and skinned his knee. Hold your daughter if she's scared of the shadows in her bedroom. Rub your son's back if he's crying so hard he can't seem to get his breath.

"You sound scared."

Acknowledge the child's feelings even if you have to guess what they are. Attempting to talk a child out of his or her feelings is ineffective medicine when combating Empathy Deficit Disorder.

"You seem frightened" is empathetic. "There's no reason to feel scared" is EDD in action. "It must feel bad not to get invited to the party" communicates understanding and caring. "There will be other parties. We can have one of our own" tells the child that his or her feelings are not important.

Lead with empathy when combating this dreaded disease. Teaching, reassuring, disciplining, explaining, and providing information can come later. When your child is in the midst of powerful emotion, telling her there is no good reason for her feelings exacerbates the problem. "I see tears in your eyes. You look sad" leads with empathy. So does "So you felt envious when she wore the new clothes."

Demonstrate understanding by telling your grieving son, "You took the loss hard. Do you want to talk or be left alone for a while?" Show him that

EDD has no place in your home by saying, "You're really concerned about that" and "It's OK to feel bad for a while."

"Don't you talk to me like that!"

Children occasionally lose control and make emotional outbursts. They say things like:

"I hate you."

"I want a different mommy."

"I wish I didn't live here."

When you're the target of such an outburst, it's easy to get defensive. Responding with anger is common. "Don't you talk to me like that!" "Who do you think you are?" and "You're really in trouble now, young lady" are often a parent's defensive response.

An alternative to being defensive often employed by angered parents is to attempt to talk children out of their feelings.

"You don't really mean that."

"You're just mad right now. You'll feel better later."

"You're just saying that."

Neither defensiveness nor talking children out of their feelings when they appear to attack us with words is helpful. Both invalidate feelings, hurt the relationship, and escalate power struggles.

Instead, ignore the words. Refuse to respond to the child's words. Go deeper. Look for the feelings below the words and use Parent Talk that responds to the child on that level.

"You must be really angry to talk to me like that."

"I can hear how hurt you are right now."

"You're so frustrated, you say mean things."

By using Parent Talk that responds to the feeling beneath the words, you act from a place of understanding. You communicate empathy and hear the hurt that lies below the hurting words. You connect at a time of attempted disconnect. You become the skilled parent so the child can have room to be the child.

"Let's talk about it."

Yes, talking with children builds connectedness. Yes, conversations cement bonding and strengthen relationships. Yes, intimacy occurs when communication is positive, uplifting, caring, and respectful. So talk with and listen to your children on a regular basis.

Are you aware that language-rich homes have been linked with success in reading and school achievement? And much of this happens before kids even register for kindergarten. Parents, the key to literacy is not located in the schoolhouse. It is found at home. If you want your children to have a literacy edge when they enter school, do the following.

- Beginning at birth, increase both the quantity and quality of conversations between you and your children.
- Use rich language. (Yes, big words for small children.) The vocabulary you use is what children have to select from when they become writers and readers.

- It's OK to use words children do not understand. Children learn words from usage. Use them often.
- Retell family stories.
- Talk about the world.
- Talk about the future.
- Ask questions that seek opinions.

Every one of us can talk to our children. And it can make a huge difference in their literacy development as well as build a solid foundation for their primary relationship, the one they have with you.

So, talk, talk, talk, and listen.

"Come here and tell me."

Are you a *come-here* or a *go-there* parent? *Come-here* messages invite children into our lives and create connectedness. *Go-there* messages send children away and result in a disconnect.

<u>Go-There Parent Talk</u>	<u>Come-Here Parent Talk</u>
Go brush your teeth.	Let's go brush teeth.
Get back in bed.	Come here and tell me what's happening.

Go clean your room.	Show me your room.
Better leave or you'll be late.	Come here so I can give you a hug.
Go put a Band-Aid on it.	Let's find a Band-Aid.
Both of you go to your rooms.	Let's gather at the kitchen to talk about this.

How do you react to commonly occurring parenting situations? Do you build closeness and a positive relationship with come-here invitations? Or do you repel children and create distance with go-there commands?

Of course, children can brush their teeth alone, and you can strengthen the experience and your parent/child bond by doing it with your young children. At some point in their lives, your children will feel babied if you brush your teeth while they're brushing theirs. They will prefer to do it alone.

We're not suggesting you do everything with your child and never send a go-there message. We are saying it's important to create a balance of go-there and come-here messages. If you don't, you could be missing wonderful opportunities to connect with your children and share with them the beauty of a warm relationship.

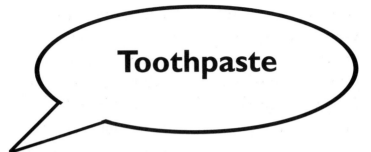

Toothpaste

Feeling stressed about parenting issues? Is anger, frustration, or irritation creeping into your language patterns? Are you hearing a divisive tone? If so, before you speak, think "toothpaste."

Communicating with your children is like using a tube of toothpaste. You have to "squeeze out" your Parent Talk slowly and thoughtfully for one important reason. As with toothpaste, once your words are out, it's impossible to put them back in.

We've all done it. You hear yourself say something to your child and wish you hadn't. It feels like it just came out. You didn't think about it. You didn't say it on purpose. And there it was, rolling off your lips as though you said it with intentionality. Maybe you heard the unwanted phrase when you were a child growing up and now you sound like your parent. Perhaps you heard it from other adults and there it is, coming out of your own mouth as if you were the originator of the word combination.

Reining in loose lips is not always easy. It demands conscious attention to your thoughts and expectations. It requires a belief that parenting has more to do with controlling ourselves than it does with controlling our children. Pay attention to what triggers you. Is it irritation, stress, sleep deprivation, hunger, whining, disowning responsibility, or excuse giving? Break the cycle by anticipating these situations. Take a deep breath, count to ten, say a silent prayer, or take a time-out. Lose those loose lips before you say something you'll regret. Stop, think, and listen.

Before you communicate anger, reprimand your child, or speak from frustration, think "toothpaste." Refuse to say something you wish you hadn't. Show your beautiful toothpaste smile instead.

"I love you" are three words all children need to hear often from their parents. Do you want those words to have real meaning to your child? Do you want them to connect one heart to another? Do you want to use these words to develop a level of intimacy in your family that communicates your heartfelt affection for your children? If so, consider strengthening *I love you* with the following suggestions.

Use eye contact. Give your children your eyes when you say, "I love you." Souls touch when meaningful eye contact is made during moments of intimacy. Touch with your eyes. It's a way of connecting that helps you bond.

Touch. A pat on the back, a hug, or a high five will add meaning to verbal expressions of love. So will a slight squeeze of the shoulder or a kiss. Take your child's hand in yours when you say, "I love you," and add a tactile component to your words.

Add nonverbal signals to your spoken message. Smile, wink, and add pleasant facial expressions to your words. Make sure the message on your face is congruent with the one coming out of your mouth.

Say "I love you" at unexpected times. Children often hear our expressions of love at familiar times. We typically say "I love you" when we're going out the door on our way to work. We say it when we end a phone conversation. "I love you" is often the last communication our children hear as we tuck them into bed at night. "I love you" at those times is often expected and certainly anticipated.

To heighten the impact of these three valuable words, use them at unexpected times. Say them in the middle of a meal, as you're driving down the road in your car, or as you stand at the kitchen sink doing dishes together.

Some children are auditory and need to hear the words "I love you." Others are tactile and need to be touched to feel loved. Still others are visual and need to see love on your face and in your actions. Why not give your children all three variations when you communicate your love?

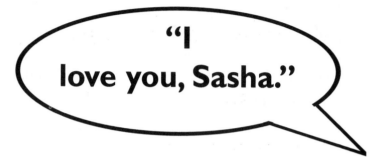

"I love you, Sasha."

The sweetest sound in any language is the sound of your own name. Names get our attention and build connectedness. Sadly, some children only hear their own names when they're in trouble. "William, you better get in here!" Add your child's name to your expression of love. "I love you, Carlos" or "Shingo, I really love you." Watch their reactions. Their facial expressions will encourage you to continue the practice of adding your child's name to "I love you."

An alternative to using names when you express love is to use the words son and daughter. These two words can add intense intimacy to your verbal expressions of love. "I love you, son" or "I love you, daughter" will create an emotion-filled statement that will invite an equally emotional response. Monitor your personal comfort level as you use these two important words. Notice your feelings as you say them, as well as the reaction you get from your children.

Remove the word *when* from your vocal communication of love. "I love you *when* you smile like that" or "*When* you choose that happy mood, I love you" sends a message to your children that your love is conditional. What children often hear is "I *only* love you *when*." To love unconditionally, say "I love you" without any stipulation attached.

Remove the word *but* from your description of love. "I love you, *but*" is usually followed by a concern, problem, or frustration.

"I love you, but you need to use deodorant."

"I love you, but you don't get to go."

"I love you, but you have to learn your multiplication tables before this weekend."

When we express our love along with a concern, we send a mixed message. When we do this, children get confused and conclude that the love part is a manipulation intended to soften them up before the real message (the concern) is delivered.

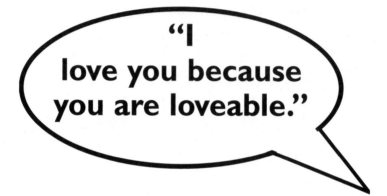

"I love you because you are loveable" is an important concept for children to learn. It helps them understand that your love is attached to no specific condition. It simply is.

Be careful not to add any other words after "because." "I love you because you are thoughtful" adds a condition that communicates conditional love. The only acceptable phrase to use with "because" is "because you are loveable."

"Because..."

Want to get more cooperation from your children? Would you like them to go along with your desires more often? Do you want more influence over their behavior? If so, you need the influence enhancer "BECAUSE."

Because is a word of influence. Advertisers and marketers use it regularly to influence our behaviors. They have learned that we agree with their suggestions more often when they give us a reason to do so. "Buy this car *because* it gets great gas mileage." "Give to this charity *because* it helps battered women get a fresh start and change their lives for the better."

Parents also can use the influence enhancer to encourage appropriate behaviors. "Whining doesn't work with me *because* it hurts my ears and I don't understand what you are really asking for." "We lay books flat on the shelf or stand them up straight *because* it hurts their spines and injures the pages to leave them open like that." "Nine o'clock is the healthy limit we have set for bedtime *because* your young body needs regular sleep so you can be alert and full of energy in the morning."

Use "because," the influence enhancer, *because* you will get less resistance to your parental suggestions. Use it *because* it works to create fewer power struggles. Use it *because* it will help you build a positive relationship with your child and move closer to becoming the parent you really want to be.

"It's Sunday night. Time for popcorn."

Family rituals are an effective way to build connectedness and positive relationships. A ritual is any activity that the family enjoys and does repeatedly. This could be as simple as having popcorn every Sunday night or as complicated as planning a special dinner once a month.

A ritual can be connected to a holiday or can occur because of a special achievement. It may require money or not. Prayers before bedtime, calling Grandma on Sunday night, and meeting Dad at the airport when he comes in from a business trip all qualify.

"Jenny got a *First*. Time to celebrate."

Chick's daughter Jenny swung her right leg forward with equal amounts of force and precision. Her foot connected squarely with the soccer ball and sent it on an arcing path over the goalie's head, under the crossbar, and into the net. The goal, her first in forty-three American Youth Soccer Organization games, was greeted with the traditional backslaps, high fives, and wide grins.

The spontaneous ninety-second celebration that followed Jenny's first goal was warm, genuine, and esteem enhancing. It recognized her individual accomplishment as well as the total team effort. But more importantly for their family, it served as a signal to activate one of their favorite family rituals, for Jenny had just achieved a *First*.

Firsts. This term holds special meaning for Chick's family and is cause for celebration. Firsts are defined as any event, success, or goal achievement that occurs for the first time. These Firsts are benchmarks in his family's lives that signal an active participation in life and a willingness to take risks. They are visible reminders of growth. As such, they deserve special recognition. Some Firsts his family has recognized include: Randy pitching a shutout; Matt learning how to read; Chick publishing the Spirit Whisperer book; Jenny getting on the honor roll; Chick doing a workshop for teachers in a foreign country; and Matt learning to ride his bike.

Their celebration of each First was done on purpose, with a specific format, for a specific reason. The family showcased Firsts by going out to dinner together. The individual who had achieved the First became the focus person. He or she chose both the time and place for the celebration.

At the appointed time the family gathered to share a meal, acknowledge the individual, and practice their collective caring. The focus person took the spotlight and told about his or her special moment, communicating feelings, reactions, impressions, or any new goals he or she had set. The rest of the family listened without interrupting the narrative.

When the focus person finished sharing, the rest of family could participate by telling what they liked about either the First or the reaction of the person who accomplished it. Informal conversation followed until the conclusion of their celebration.

Celebrating Firsts helped Chick's family achieve two important goals simultaneously. The activity allowed them to connect as a family as well as celebrate the uniqueness of the person being honored.

We hope you will steal this idea and use it with your family. But remember, Chick's family did it first.

"Look what I bought you."

A neighbor recently purchased a four-hundred-dollar sandbox for his young children. How can anyone spend four hundred dollars on a sandbox? you might wonder. Simple. It's a state-of-the-art sandbox with a swing set and slide attached to it. It's high quality through and through.

With all due respect to the neighbor (who loves his children and has the best of intentions when making major purchases for them, we're sure), children do not need a four-hundred-dollar sandbox. What they do need is the experience of going out to the backyard with their parents and building a sandbox. They need to hold boards together while we pound, and do the pounding while we take a turn holding the boards together. They need to get a sliver and have it removed and bandaged. They need to help us sand the boards so slivers are kept to a minimum. They need to rub shoulders with us, sweat with us, smell us, see us, touch us, and hear us. They need the experience of *building* a sandbox much more than they need the sandbox.

So when investing in your children, invest in experiences, not in things. Instead of buying another stuffed giraffe for them, take them to the zoo and let them experience a real giraffe up close. Buying a new fishing pole is fine, but using it is better. Take your children fishing.

Have your children seen a horse, touched a horse, ridden a horse? Purchasing the Disney movie *Spirit* is one thing; getting in touch with the spirit of a live horse and feeling its breath on your face is another.

We'll say it again: Children need experiences and TIME with us more than they need things. Give children what they really want from their parents: your presence, not your presents.

"Let's go for a walk."

All children spell love T-I-M-E.

If you want to build a positive relationship with your children, you have to give them your time. Ride a bike, wash the car, read a book, or hang out in the kitchen together. What you do is less important. That you do it together is more important.

- Take a blanket and pillow outdoors at night. Count the stars. Look for satellites.
- Take a walk in the woods. Look for animal tracks. Notice trees and flowers.
- Play catch, shoot baskets, volley a ball or hit a badminton bird. Challenge each other to see how long you can keep the ball going rather than seeing who can score the most points.
- Have a water balloon fight. Get wet. Get wild. Get silly. Get with your children.
- Catch fireflies and put them in a jar. Later, let them go.
- Go to a parade. Get there early. Stake out your territory with folding chairs and blankets.

Invite a friend or relative.

- Pick cherries, strawberries, blueberries, raspberries, corn, apples, beans, or a vegetable or fruit of your choice. Get stained, dirty, and sweaty.
- Sit around a campfire. Talk. Listen. Roast marshmallows.
- Plant a tree.
- Write and send postcards–from home or from out of state.
- Clean a closet. Collect unused and outgrown clothes. Donate them to an appropriate charity.
- Take a trip to the library. Let your children choose several books. You choose some, too. Read to your children over the next several weeks.
- Go on a photo journey. Allow each family member to take a set number of photos. Create a family album with the developed photos.
- Do loving service. Bake cookies for a serviceman or servicewoman. Mow the grass for an elderly couple. Pick up litter from a roadside picnic area.
- Go garage-sale hopping with five dollars in your pocket. Give your children a similar amount. Come home when everyone has spent all their money.
- Walk in the rain. Sing in the rain. Skip through

puddles. Take your shoes off. Take your adult-hood off.

- If you live in the country, go to a big city and walk around. If you live in a city, go to the country and walk around.
- Check out a college campus.
- Make popsicles with Kool-Aid and toothpicks.
- Visit a post office. Mail a letter.
- Bring out old photo albums. Take turns saying, "I remember when . . ."
- Cut and paste. Staple and glue. Color and paint. Make a mess. Then clean up.

Let your children experience a farm, a sky-scraper, a fire engine, a campground, or a foreign country. Let them smell a flower, look for birds, feed ducks, or bake cookies. Help them find a four-leaf clover, shuck corn, wash the car, or open a savings account. Whatever you do, remember to do it TOGETHER.

"Let me get off the computer so I can give you my full attention."

Many people are proud of their ability to multitask these days. They brag about how they can pay the bills, watch television, and help their kids with homework all at the same time. If building relationship with your children or teaching them how to focus on a specific task is of any interest to you, multitasking won't get you there.

Multitasking that includes children sends them an unspoken message: "You are not important enough for me to give you my full attention."

Sondra McCarty was reading the paper when her teen came home from school. She immediately put down the newspaper and focused on her son. "Tough day?" she asked. "Yes," he responded. "The English test was a monster. Not sure how I did on it. I won't know until Monday." When her cell phone rang, Sondra put it on vibrate without answering it. "It must be kind of tough to have to wait three days to find out how you did," she empathized, continuing a conversation that would last fifteen more minutes.

Carlos Montoya played chess with his daughter every night after dinner. This night, as he contemplated which chess piece to move next, his thoughts were scattered. He remembered the colleague he had chosen to confront earlier in the day. He thought about three bills that he was unable to pay this week, hoped his wife would be in an amorous mood later, and planned out his morning presentation in his mind. When his daughter said, "It's your move again, Dad," he came back to reality and realized that even though he was sitting at the table with her, he wasn't present.

Carlos centered himself by focusing on his breathing. He knew that was one way to get out of his mind and back to the present moment. He looked at his daughter's face and said a short prayer of gratitude to be blessed with this moment. For the rest of the game Carlos ignored the effort of his mind to take him away from the table and his daughter. He remained present.

Multitasking prevents us from giving our children our attention, our availability, our mindfulness, our closeness, and our time. We're suggesting that you avoid the urge to multitask and strive instead to stay focused on the moment at hand. When you sit with your children, whether it's to play a game or read a book, give them your undivided attention.

"I GUESS WE CAN SKIP 'HOW DO YOUR CHILDREN GET ALONG.'"

"What kind of treats shall we get for our family New Year's party?"

Some parents see New Year's Eve as an opportunity to get away from the family to celebrate in private or with friends. Going out to dinner, attending parties, and emptying bottles seems to be the order of the day and night. Consider another alternative, one that can help your family grow closer. Spend New Year's Eve together. It's an ideal time to celebrate connectedness, reflect on the past year, and look ahead to the future.

Deciding what treats to purchase, shopping together, and decorating could occupy much of your family's time on the day that leads up to the big evening. Dinner and card games might fill the early evening. When interest in games dies down, assemble in the living room, sit in a circle, and begin the most meaningful part of your New Year's Eve together: Topic Talk.

Topics are ideas family members dream up to help structure your conversation. One family member suggests a topic like "a new friend I made this year" or "my favorite song this year." Each member then takes a turn responding orally to the topic, telling as much as he or she chooses. Listeners do simply that–listen, until everyone has responded. When each person has had an opportunity to respond to the topic, you can ask questions or elaborate on your remarks. Some topics that could help you connect with each other and reflect on the previous year include: my favorite book this year; something I did that I'm proud of; something I wish I could do over; my favorite place I visited this year; something I bought for myself; something I did for others.

At eleven o'clock, end Topic Talk and make a list of goals. Each person can take turns reading their goals and telling why they are important to them. Get a volunteer to act as recorder and take down all goal statements as they're dictated. The goals are then put away until your next New Year's Eve celebration.

As the time nears midnight, turn on the TV and count down the minutes and seconds. The traditional hugs, kisses, and noisemaking are important to include in your celebration.

Adapt this idea to fit you and your family. Gather your family together and lead off the New Year's celebration by sharing your goal for the new year: to promote togetherness and build family spirit.

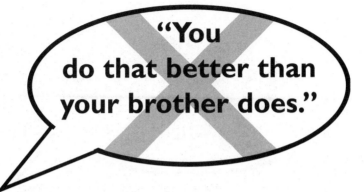

"You do that better than your brother does."

Want to create a lot of sibling rivalry in your family? Want to create strain in your children's relationship with one another? Begin by comparing them to one another and let them know that you're doing it. Say things like, "Your brother never acts that way," and "If your sister can do it, why can't you?"

Holding one child up as the model and using that model to encourage better behavior on the part of the sibling is a sure way to create resentment and divisiveness among your children. It is a relationship buster.

Another way to destroy your children's relationship with one another is to ask your kids to spy. Tell your son, "I want to know if your sister uses the phone while I'm gone." Tell the younger child, "If he splashes you again, let me know." Inform your daughter, "The computer is off limits while I'm gone. Your brother will be watching you to see if you follow the rules."

If you want to increase sibling rivalry in your family, buy and play many competitive games that require one winner and many losers. Focus strongly on the importance of winning and downplay the process of playing, learning, and having fun. This way your children who have lost can fight back by playing a different game behind your back. The new game is called *getting even.*

Create even more unhealthy competition in your family by designing artificial challenges to manipulate a desired behavior, such as seeing who can get ready for bed first. Use lots of competitive Parent Talk, including, "The last one up the stairs is a rotten egg," or "The first one with their coat on gets to pick where they want to sit."

"This doesn't fit your sister anymore. It'll be perfect for you."

Another way to promote tension between siblings is to always give the younger child hand-me-downs. This ritual, if done often, can create a feeling of being a secondhand person or less important than the child who gets the new things. When this occurs, the younger one often strives to be first or get more attention in negative ways.

Yes, the economics in many families make hand-me-downs a necessity. In these cases make sure the younger child gets something new occasionally and the older one gets some passed-on clothing as well.

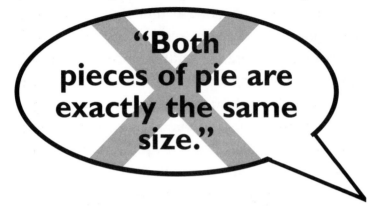

"Both pieces of pie are exactly the same size."

Parents often bend over backward in an attempt to be fair. Their belief is that if they don't treat their children exactly the same, it will promote jealousy and strain. They are mistaken. Attempting to be fair often results in increased competitiveness and ill-feeling among children.

So parents frequently go to great lengths to make sure that everyone has the same amount of orange drink in their cup or the same number of french fries on their plate. They work hard to cut equal amounts of cake.

First, it's not possible to cut equal amounts of cake. Second, even if you did, children don't always see it that way. An effort to be consistently fair will create an atmosphere where your children are constantly checking to make sure they have the same or slightly more than the other child. This does not promote the healthy relationships you want to foster in your family.

Many unfair things happen in life. One person gets a ticket while speeding, another does not. Both were going the same speed. One child's parent is deployed in a combat zone, his classmate's parent is not. One child's mother has breast cancer, her friend's mother is healthy. So how are you going to deal with that level of unfairness? What verbal skills are you going to use to explain those situations? Read on.

Children of all ages ask serious questions about serious issues. You may have a spouse in the war zone, one with a serious illness, or be facing a family financial crisis.

"Are you going to die?"

"How come Mommy throws up all the time?"

"Do you have to spend all your time in bed?"

"Is Daddy going to get killed?"

"Are we going to be poor?"

If you or your spouse is dealing with a serious

illness or a stint in the military, or if you are both out of work, stress and anxiety is a given. The demands of caring for your sick spouse and your children or dealing with financial and safety worries can generate an emotional strain that is difficult to manage.

Individuals do not get a serious illness or experience a major life change, *families* do. Whether we're talking about cancer, Alzheimers, a heart condition, deployment in a foreign country, or loss of a job, the entire family is affected. Schedules change. So do parenting responsibilities. Typical daily concerns become magnified and are more difficult to work through when a crisis occurs in the family.

Whether you're the one facing a personal crisis or are the caregiving spouse, your own emotional issues and daily concerns increase. In addition, you are now expected to nurture children who are unsure, fearful, and lonely and who are being asked to cope with uncertainty and change in their own young lives.

How do you handle it? How do you respond to their fears when some days you aren't even sure how to handle your own? How do you answer their questions when the only thing you know for sure is that you don't have all the answers and are living in the midst of uncertainty yourself? How do you deal with your child's strong emotions when you're caught up in your own intense feelings? What's a concerned, loving parent to do?

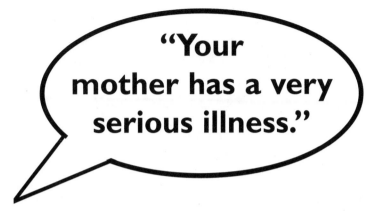

"Your mother has a very serious illness."

Tell the truth. Give your children accurate information regardless of their age. Yes, using age-appropriate language that takes the developmental level of the child into account is important. You don't say the same things to a teenager as you do to a two-year-old. If your four-year-old asks, "Will Daddy die?", you don't give her a statistical analysis of the number of people who have survived lung cancer. You say, "We don't think so. With cancer, sometimes people die, but we know that Daddy, his doctor, and all of us are doing everything we can to help him get well." Answer accurately within the child's field of understanding.

If your spouse is in a correctional facility, do not tell your children that he's working out of town. Tell them, "Your father made some mistakes and now he has to make amends. He wasn't completely honest and now he has to live with the outcomes of his choices."

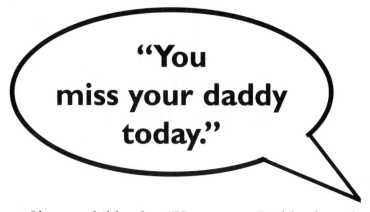

"You miss your daddy today."

If your child asks, "How come Daddy doesn't seem to care about me anymore?", this is not the time to focus on the content of the message. It is not helpful at this time to reassure your child that his father does care or work to convince him that his feelings are wrong. Focus your attention instead on responding to the feelings that are stated or implied. Say, "You're missing the playtime you used to have with your dad today," or "It feels lonely to have your dad spend so much time in the hospital, doesn't it?"

The feeling that your child is communicating is more important than the surface content of his or her words. Children are starving for feeling recognition. Satisfy their hunger by helping them focus on their feelings without attempting to talk them out of those feelings.

> "Mommy had an important operation. The doctor, who was trained at the University of Michigan, removed one of her breasts. Her chances of survival are 76 percent. Ten years ago the survival rate was 20 percent, so you can see that many advances have been made in medicine since you were born."

Don't give children more information than they ask for. If your seven-year-old wants to know why she can't jump into Mommy's lap, it isn't necessary to explain the recent surgical procedure, technological nuances, or the inner workings of the healing body. After acknowledging your child's feeling tone as suggested, give her a simple answer: "It's difficult to respond to quick movements when healing is taking place, and Mom needs to be touched gently right now so she can heal." If your child wants to know more, she'll ask.

"Let's make a get well card for mommy."

Help your children stay connected to the absent parent whether they are in a hospital, a jail, or on a foreign battlefield. Encourage your child to write letters and make drawings or get well cards for their mother or father. Having a regular communication time set aside–Sunday night, for example–is helpful. Get out your special Daddy/Mommy Communication Box that contains paper, envelopes, stamps, special pens, stickers, postcards, and so on. Model for your children the importance of ongoing communication with their missing parent.

Don't deny the severity of the situation. Children have built-in bull detectors. They can tell when you're not being honest with them. They can sense when things are tense. They pick up on your moods and overhear you talking to others. Be straight with them about the possibilities inherent in the current situation that you're facing if they ask.

On the other hand, it's not necessary to talk about every possible negative outcome. If your children want to know, they'll ask. Keep the severity warnings to a bare minimum.

Use Parent Talk that focuses on the helpers. Let your children know that when problems arise, the helpers come. There are many helpers in our society. Doctors and nurses are helpers. Concerned neighbors and relatives are helpers. Debt relief counselors are helpers. Many people see God as their number one helper.

Show your children how God and people are helping you and your family. Be appreciative of the helpers and let your children hear you express it.

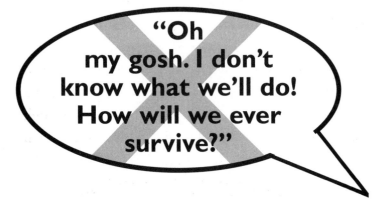

"Oh my gosh. I don't know what we'll do! How will we ever survive?"

Do not become hysterical in your children's presence or vent on, confide in, or use them as your support system. Don't expect your children to take care of your emotional state. If you need to vent or share your fears and worries, turn to a member of the clergy, a counselor, friends, or relatives. It is not your children's job to be *your* support system. It is your job to be *their* support system.

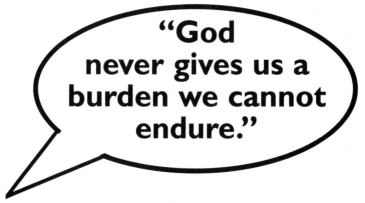

Do tell your children about your faith. Your beliefs and your family's beliefs are important at this time. Pray with your children regularly if that fits with your belief. Use this opportunity to help them learn that you trust God, and model for them how your faith sustains you in time of need.

Tell your children about family strength and the history of your family character.

"We have a strong family and we'll make it through."

"We'll be able to handle it together."

"I know you can handle it."

"I know you can handle it" is a form of encouragement that communicates your respect for your children's ability to manage their own lives. While you cannot guarantee that life will always give them exactly what they want, you can help them feel secure in their ability and the family's ability to cope with whatever circumstances present themselves.

DIVORCE

When you said the words "I do" on your wedding day, the idea of divorce probably never entered your mind. Nor was it even a fleeting thought when you witnessed the birth of your first child. Chances are it never occurred to you at those times that one day you would be another statistic in the over 50 percent of marriages that end in divorce.

And yet here you are, considering divorce or separation, or perhaps you're already divorced. Today you find yourself dealing with issues of dating, visitation schedules, and feelings of animosity toward your spouse. You know that divorce is not the best situation for your children, but things have progressed too far to turn back now.

What do you do at this point to protect your children? How do you help them minimize the negative effects of a divorce? What do you say to them and how do you say it? How you handle yourself throughout the divorce process and the months that follow can be a determining factor in how well your children handle the struggles that divorce can bring.

Divorce does not have to be a devastating end to your family. It can mark the beginning of a new family for you and your children. Focus on creating a new life together. Hold onto some of the traditions of the past and look for opportunities to create new traditions, new routines, and a newfound joy in being together. Show your children how to divorce gracefully by eliminating the negative Parent Talk that you may be tempted to use with them during this critical time.

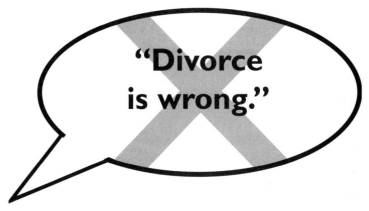

Before you say one word about your impending divorce to your children, you must first put your morals aside. You don't have to give them up. Just put them on a shelf during this important time in your children's lives. If you haven't already talked with them about your religious point of view or what you believe about divorce, this isn't the time to bring it up. Save the moral and religious discussion for a later date. You will have many opportunities to talk with them about your point of view after the stress of the divorce process is over.

Making statements such as "Divorce is wrong," "Divorce is against God's word," or "I don't believe in divorce" sends the message to your children that their other parent is at fault. When this type of Parent Talk is used, it positions one parent as being right and the other as being wrong. Children are then put in the middle between Mom and Dad, having to choose between right and wrong. This is not a healthy position in which to place your child. It is not a choice your children should ever have to make.

Your moral stance doesn't change the fact that a divorce is taking place. Your belief about how wrong a divorce is won't stop the divorce from happening. Your focus at this time should not be on giving a moral lesson or fixing blame. Focus instead on your children and helping them through this transition time in their life. Moving through a divorce with dignity and grace is the key to keeping it from affecting your children adversely.

What children hear their parents say about each other and the behavior they see their parents exhibit toward each other is what makes a divorce devastating or not. How you talk about your partner and act toward him or her as well as what you say to your children is what will be taken to heart and remembered for a lifetime. Your Parent Talk as well as your accompanying behavior will determine the effect a divorce has on your children.

"IF WE DON'T HAVE ROOM FOR ALL OUR PARENTS ON THE FRONT, MISS SIMS, CAN WE USE THE BACK?"

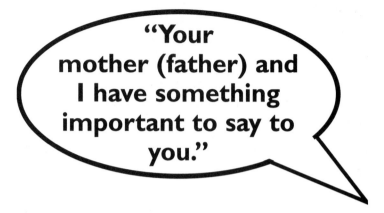

"**Your mother (father) and I have something important to say to you.**"

Once you have set your moral stance and your belief system aside, it's time to sit down with your children and talk to them about what is happening. They already know that something is going on. Honor their intelligence and help them to cope during this stressful time in their lives by creating an open and honest dialogue. If you don't tell them what you're planning to do and how you're going to do it, their imaginations will run wild and fill in the blanks. Their anxiety will skyrocket, and disruptive behaviors may emerge.

Call a family meeting. During the meeting you have the opportunity to send your children a powerful message, a message that will make a lasting impression, a message that must be delivered together. *Yes,* in spite of all your differences, disagreements, arguments, and fights, you and your spouse must sit down *together* and talk with your children. This may be the hardest thing you both do together during your dissolution of the marriage, and it is by far the most important.

Sitting down together, as adults, in the midst of this turmoil sends an important message. You are saying to your children that we, your parents, are going to keep you first in our thoughts and minds as we move forward. You are letting your children know that they still come first.

This family meeting also provides direction and sets the tone for what is to come. A divorce doesn't have to be a terrible thing. It's a new beginning in which the adults can get back to living a full, rich life. When the adults are living healthy, happy lives, the children benefit. Ultimately, children want to see their parents happy. The direction and tone of this meeting is about how you all are going to get on with the adventure of creating peaceful, relaxed, fulfilling lives.

"**This will only take a minute.**"

This is not a sentence you say aloud to your children. It's one you say to yourself to remind yourself that once you begin this conversation you have one minute or less to get your message across the way you want it to be heard before your children's emotions kick in and prevent them from being able to hear you. Just so you're clear on this, we will say it again. You have one minute to make the most important points you and your spouse want to make before your children are so caught up in emotion that their hearing becomes distorted.

The two of you need to plan ahead of time precisely what is going to be said in those crucial seconds. Practice so you can keep it under one minute. If you talk for longer than that, your children's emotions will take over and they'll begin to tune you out. Once that happens, they will likely start building ideas in their heads to make sense of what is going on.

Keep this one minute message short, sweet, and to the point.

"Your father [mother] and I have decided to change our family structure. We've decided to live apart. We will be leaving each other. We are not leaving you. We both love you very much. Your father and I will still be spending a lot of time with you. We are having a lot of trouble getting along with each other. It has nothing to do with you. Sometimes you will see your father or me angry or frustrated. It's important for you to know that it is not about you. The negative feelings are between your dad and me. We are planning on creating a more peaceful life for us and for you."

Once you have delivered your initial message, shift the focus to the children. The bulk of the family meeting should be spent on listening, allowing your children to share their feelings, and communicating your empathy with them.

While the initial part of this meeting is only one minute in length, the remainder of the session can last as long as your children need it to. Your parenting responsibility here is to allow them to have and express their feelings. Your children need to hear and see during this meeting that both you and your spouse intend to keep your commitment to being parents. You don't have to live together or even be married for that to happen.

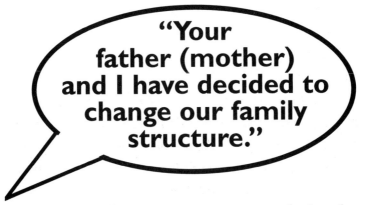

"Your father (mother) and I have decided to change our family structure."

The above phrase is important to use during the sixty-second beginning of your family meeting. The truth is, the family structure is *changing*, it's not over. And it will be different. It will bring change for everyone, whether that change is desired or not.

"We will be getting a divorce."

Avoid using the word *divorce* during the initial meeting and throughout the rest of the divorce process. Children already have a preconceived notion of what divorce means and what it looks like based on what they hear from their friends and see in the lives of others. When they hear the word *divorce,* they will immediately shift to what they think is going to take place. Your goal is to reassure them that you are changing the family structure, not your care and concern for them.

The structure is changing to a situation in which Mom and Dad will be living in different homes. It will, however, be changing as little as possible for the children. They will still go to the same school and play with the same friends. They will still have a bedroom, and perhaps two bedrooms. They will have special time with Mom and special time with Dad. They will be taken care of in pretty much the same way they've been taken care of up to this point. The focus will continue to remain on providing them with all they need to grow up to be fabulous, healthy, responsible people in the world.

The structure of the family will change, but the care and concern for your children will not. Parents don't need to be in the same home, living under the same roof, to provide their children with what is needed to help them become caring, confident, successful adults.

"We are leaving each other. We are not leaving you."

Every young child has abandonment fears. Older children can feel it as well, although often not as strongly as the younger ones. During the time of separation and/or divorce proceedings it's helpful to tell your children and show them that they are not being abandoned. Reassuring Parent Talk is necessary here.

"We both love you very much."

"Your father and I will still be spending a lot of time with you."

"We are having a lot of trouble getting along with each other. It has nothing to do with you."

"Sometimes you will see your mother or me angry or frustrated. It's important for you to know that it is not about you. The negative feelings are between your mom and me."

Your reassuring Parent Talk has to be backed up by action if it is to be believed by your children. They hear you say the words, "I will still be spending a lot of time with you," but if your behavior doesn't match those words, your actions will drown them out.

"LET'S HAVE THE COUNSELOR TALK TO EDDIE ABOUT HIS PARENTS' DIVORCE."

During times of relationship crisis, when emotions run raw and frustration seems endless, remember that your children are also experiencing new emotions that accompany change and uncertainty. They are concerned, fearful, angry, anxious, and worried. While it's important to *tell* them, "We both love you very much," it is more important to *show* them you love them very much.

More hugs, phone calls, e-mails, attention, and time invested in them are important at this time. You can say, "Your mother and I are leaving each other. We are not leaving you," but the critical piece is demonstrating to your children that you are not leaving them physically, emotionally, or spiritually

"**We are planning on creating a more peaceful life for all of us.**"

It is very likely that the home environment has been stressful and tense in the recent past. When an environment is stressful, it's difficult for children to sleep, learn and stay on track developmentally. Your children have been feeling the tension. They know something has been going on. They are uncomfortable and prefer life to be peaceful and fun. Chances are they've been hoping you would do something to create a more stable situation.

Reassure your children that your goal is to create peace in your life and in their lives, too. Children want their parents to be happy. They know that when Mom and Dad are happy and at peace, life is peaceful for them as well.

As you move forward through the divorce process, focus on creating a more tranquil life for you and your children. Remind them frequently that this is your goal.

"Did you know Bobby's parents don't live together?"

"Angie is spending the weekend at her father's and won't be able to come for a sleepover this week."

"Jimmy's last name is different than his mom's because his mom and dad aren't married to each other."

Children hear about divorce from their friends at school and in day care. They overhear conversations you have with family members or neighbors. They see divorce being depicted in movies and on television shows. They are aware of what others are saying about divorce.

Where do you want your children to get their divorce information? Do you prefer they get it from you or from friends and TV?

Earlier we recommended that talking about your religious point of view and your personal beliefs about divorce not be done while you are in the middle of a divorce or separation yourself. We stand by that. That doesn't mean, however, that you never share your religious beliefs and moral stance on divorce with your children.

Clearly, it is your job as a parent to help your children make sense of the world in which they live. One of your major roles is to clarify information, dispel myths, share your morals, and present your religious point of view. And that includes your thoughts and attitudes about divorce. The key to sharing this type of information with children lies in the timing. While you're in the middle of a divorce isn't the best time to communicate it. You and your children will be better served if you await the teachable moment.

Topics will come up that are a perfect lead-in for you to provide this much-needed information. You don't need to prepare a speech or have a "big talk" about divorce. Instead, be alert for small moments that give you an opportunity to teach your children about love, relationships, intimacy, marriage, and divorce. Your children will ask questions or bring up topics that will provide an opening for you to talk to them briefly about divorce. Keep your discussion short and to the point. Remember, you will have more opportunities. You won't need to cover everything in one conversation.

Use those teachable moments to talk to your children about marriage and divorce. If you don't, they'll be getting their information somewhere else. Better to let it come from you.

"We're staying together until you're out of school."

If you stay in a horrible relationship just for the kids, you're doing your family a tremendous disservice. If the present situation is that untenable and you've exhausted all the help options available, the best thing to do is get out. It's absolutely unhealthy for kids to live in an environment of prolonged and continuous fighting. They will resent you for keeping them there.

Yet, do consider the timing. You don't want to make a divorce your child's high school graduation present or the biggest memory she takes away from that day.

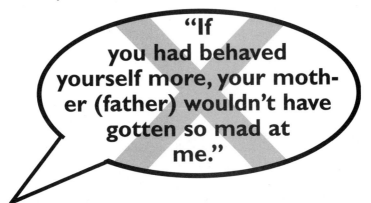

"If you had behaved yourself more, your mother (father) wouldn't have gotten so mad at me."

This is thinly veiled child abuse. Your child is NOT responsible for your relationship problems with your partner. Using Parent Talk that hints that your children are in some way responsible for your divorce or separation wounds their spirit and slashes their soul. Regardless of what they have done or said, putting responsibility on them is totally inappropriate.

Remember, a divorce takes place between the two married people in the relationship. Although divorce affects the children, you are not divorcing them. You are divorcing the person to whom you are married.

Even when you assure children that they are not

responsible for the marriage breakup, most children believe they *are* somehow responsible. They think to themselves, "If I'd only been better, it wouldn't have happened," or "If I had just done something different, things would be OK with Mom and Dad."

If you really believe that your children are responsible for your divorce, then something is in need of repair in your parent-child relationship. Turn to a counselor, member of the clergy, or school personnel. Do it now. You and your children are worth it.

"Your mother is a tramp."

"Your father is a deadbeat."

"Gutless. That's what your father is."

"She's a liar. Don't you know that?"

Of course you're mad at your ex-partner. Yes, he probably did dishonorable deeds, chose some hurtful behaviors, and appears to you as selfish, noncaring, and spiteful. Still, name-calling in front of your children is inexcusable. Regardless of what he has done and how you feel about him, remember that this person is still your children's father.

If your ex-wife has had an affair or done other mean things to you, it is not your place to tell the children about her behavior. Saying hurtful things to the children about their mother does not hit the intended target, your ex. It hits and hurts the ones you love the most, your children.

Name-calling usually stems from feelings of anger and disgust. You have a right to feel angry and to express that anger. If you need to vent, find a supportive ear somewhere else. That is not your children's role. Be careful that you do not vent within earshot of them. Overhearing you make negative comments about their mother or father carries the same weight with your children as hearing those comments said directly.

Stay in control of your angry feelings when you're talking to or around your children. Attempting to knock your ex down in this way doesn't bring you up in their eyes. When they hear you using angry words about their other parent, they can see and feel the discrepancy in what you're saying and how they're feeling. They begin to distrust your words and fear that you may be making similar comments about them and their behavior. Their suspicion damages your relationship with them.

Children need to look up to their parents. You and, yes, your ex are the two most important people in their lives. For years they have looked to both of you for comfort, support, encouragement, and direction. They will continue to do so even after the divorce. Your speaking about their father or mother with words that are meant to wound only decreases the likelihood that they will look up to you in the future.

"Is your father seeing anyone?"

"What did your mom do last night?"

"Whose truck was that parked in your drive-way?"

"Does he stay overnight?"

Do not put your children in the role of informant. It is not their job to keep you updated on events and happenings involving your estranged partner. They are not conduits of information to be pumped for information. Keep them out of the middle of your relationship problems and off the witness stand.

When you use Parent Talk that requires your children to report to you and keep you informed about your ex, you're asking them to betray someone they love. They're caught in the difficult position of having to supply you with information or lie in an attempt to protect their other parent. They have to decide what might be appropriate information to tell and what information Mom or Dad might not want you to know. This is not a decision that a child needs to be making.

If there is information that you feel you really need or want to know, go to the source. Be an adult and ask your ex the questions you want answered. He or she has the right to decide what they want to tell you. If your ex isn't forthcoming with the answers, sit tight. Refrain from pumping your children for information. It's quite possible that the answer will come to you without your ever having to ask your children.

The main focus of your communication with your ex should be about your children, their development, and their continued care. Questions that don't pertain to the kids may not be any of your business. When tempted to ask your children a question about their mom or dad, ask yourself a question first. Ask whether the answer will benefit your children or yourself. Be honest with yourself at this point. If the question only benefits you, let it go.

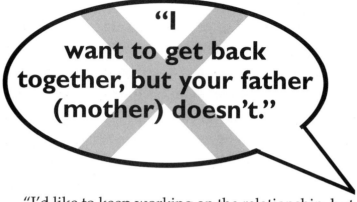

"I want to get back together, but your father (mother) doesn't."

"I'd like to keep working on the relationship, but your dad doesn't care anymore."

"Your mom's the one that doesn't want me living here."

"If I had my way, we'd all be one big happy family again."

The statements above may well be true from your point of view, but verbalizing them to your children is nothing more than a play for sympathy. They are subtle attempts to fix blame and make the other parent look bad. You are trying to place yourself in a positive light, as the only one who wants to keep the family together.

If it's really true that you want to get back together but the other person doesn't, explore your role in how the relationship has gotten to the point where it is now. Tell your partner directly that you want to get back together and work on correcting the mistakes you made in the relationship. Keep in mind that your children have no place in that negotiation process.

If you want to gain your children's affection as you go through a separation or divorce, make the transition with grace. Approach your partner with a loving heart, even when you are angry. Model for your children how to separate and move on in a relationship without wounding the spirit of another. Show your children how to have an open heart even when you don't want what another person wants. If the divorce or separation is inevitable, gift your children with the best divorce or separation possible. Divorce or separate gracefully.

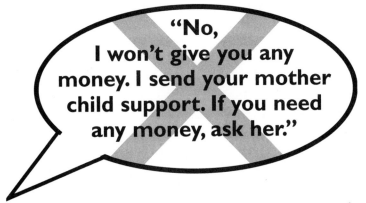

"No, I won't give you any money. I send your mother child support. If you need any money, ask her."

Your children do not need to know how much child support you pay and when you pay it. A child's request for money is not a request to be told about the family budget or about how much you pay for child support. Neither is it a request to hear about your financial troubles.

If the money is not available, and there are times in nondivorce situations when this is also true, tell them that the money isn't available right now without mentioning how much you pay for child support. Talk with your children about what they want to do with the money. Help them create a plan on how to get the money they need.

The purpose of child support is to make available a percentage of the finances needed for everyday living. Your children need far more than what child support provides. They need extra love, extra attention, and, yes, extra money on occasion.

Don't get caught up in the financial end of your relationship with your children. Be careful not to attempt to buy their love with money. Instead, show your love with time and attention.

"We'll have to do that another time. Something came up."

"My boss called me in at the last minute. I couldn't pass up the overtime."

"How about we do the zoo next time you come? I have to finish this project."

When it's your evening or weekend to be with your kids, adjust your schedule so that you can give them your full attention. This may mean skipping the golf outing, rescheduling poker night, missing softball practice, or changing your hours at work.

"SINCE THE DIVORCE, I'VE HAD SOLE CUSTODY OF MOTHER."

Create the time so that you can be present in your children's life.

When it's your weekend and you don't spend it with your kids, they feel rejected. The message they get is that something has become very important to you and that very important thing is not them. Is that the message you want to send to your children? If not, then choose to make your time with them a priority. Demonstrate to them that their time with you is the last thing to get cancelled.

If you're scheduled to have parenting time with your children and you don't show up, or you call at the last minute with a change of plans, your kids feel abandoned. If you take them to their grandparents' house for the day while you go on a golf outing, the kids question their importance to you. If you say to your daughter, "We can do that the next time we're together," and when next week arrives you don't do it, your integrity falls under suspicion.

When you have scheduled parenting time, keep it. When you say you're going to do something together next time, do it. Your children remember, and they build an image of you based on your actions. What image of you do you want them to hold?

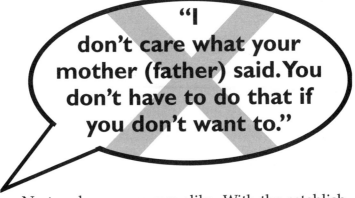

"I don't care what your mother (father) said. You don't have to do that if you don't want to."

No two homes are run alike. With the establishment of two separate homes comes the establishment of two sets of rules. The goal is to create as much consistency as possible between the rules at your house and your ex-spouse's house. Arriving at mutual agreement on issues of bedtime, homework structure, video game use and television viewing and basic rules of respect for others' boundaries is important.

While consistency is valuable, the reality is that it's difficult for many divorced couples to achieve. It takes setting aside your anger, resentment, and feelings of revenge and coming to mutual conclusions about important issues that affect your children. It takes two people behaving like adults focusing on what is best for their children. It takes honest, open, and direct Parent Talk from one parent to the other.

To say to your children, "I don't care what your mother said. You don't have to do that if you don't want to," begins to create an imbalance in the structure that children need, especially in times of divorce. The implication is that they don't have to listen to their other parent, that she doesn't know what she's talking about, and that it's OK if the child defies the parent's authority.

"I don't care what your mother said" is your effort to exert power over your ex by weakening her power with the children. You're attempting to undermine her authority and are using the children to get back at her. This is not their job. Putting them in this position gives them a sense of power that is focused in the wrong direction. Children's power needs to stay focused on managing their own behavior as they learn to make safe, caring, conscious choices.

If you really don't think the children should have to do whatever their other parent told them to do, take it up with your ex. Find out what was really behind the request or disciplinary strategy. If it's not a strategy you use in your home, talk to the children about how you handle similar situations at your house. Explain the differences in the approach each parent has taken, helping them see the outcome of their choices and the effect it has on them regardless of the house in which they reside.

"I'm going to start dating."

The time may come when you will start dating again. Many people don't feel like getting into another relationship while in the midst of a divorce. Others start dating right away. That decision is yours.

Explain the dating process to your children. Tell them you may have to date several people before you find the right one for you. Teach them how to do the dating game by living an effective dating life yourself.

Since you may date several people during this stage of your life, consider introducing your children to your date without involving them much at the beginning of a relationship. Some people you may only date once or twice. It's not a good idea to let children interact and build a relationship with your dates until they're likely to be around more regularly.

"I want you to like him."

Don't push your children into creating relationships with your new boyfriend. Allow the relationship to evolve naturally, over time. Give your children time, space, and flexibility to adjust to the new situation.

"We're getting married."

Tyler and Ginny decided to get married and blend their families. So they immediately told both sets of children. Although the couple had been dating for a year, all four of the children were shocked. They had no warning.

"We are *thinking* about getting married" would have been more effective Parent Talk at this point. *Thinking about it* would not have seemed as definite to the children. It would have given the appearance that everyone's opinion would be taken into account before the final decision was made.

"Katrina will be coming over more often because I enjoy being with her."

LONG before you decide to remarry, begin the dialogue about the possible future family life. Tell your children, "My life is good since I met Katrina," or "I sure am having fun with Katrina." This style of Parent Talk sends out subtle clues that begin to prepare the children for what might eventually occur.

When they hear, "I enjoy being with Katrina and am planning on spending more time with her," they can create a clear picture of the direction in which the relationship is heading. They don't have to do any guesswork. They are then less likely to be surprised by a major announcement later on.

"Roberto and I are enjoying each other a lot."

"I'm going to be dating Christine on a regular basis."

"Maryanne and I are growing closer together."

When you use Parent Talk that keeps your children informed about the direction and seriousness of your relationship, it will not be a major shock to them when you announce, "Roger has asked me to marry him and I said yes."

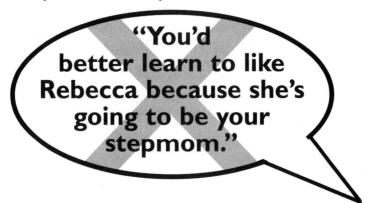

"You'd better learn to like Rebecca because she's going to be your stepmom."

"Rebecca's son is coming over this weekend and I want you to take him to the party with you on Saturday night."

"Please invite her children to share your toys."

"We've planned a family outing so you two teens can grow closer together."

"He's going to be living with us, so I want you to be close to him."

Please do not push your children into creating relationships with your new spouse-to-be or their children. Allow those relationships to evolve slowly and naturally over time. Give your children the time, space, and flexibility they need to adjust to the new situation.

A relationship that is not left to grow of its own accord will be forced and artificial. Your spouse-to-be and your children are individual beings who are free to admire and regard highly people of their own choice. When you push to have them come together, there is a natural tendency for them to push back to keep that desired closeness from happening.

Your children's relationship with your new partner will not be the same as yours. They will see him or her differently than you do. Respect those differences. The stepchildren from each half of your new relationship may or may not desire to be friends. Respect that. Yes, everyone under the roof needs to demonstrate basic respect for one another. And that will happen best when you allow their relationships to develop at their own pace and in their own way.

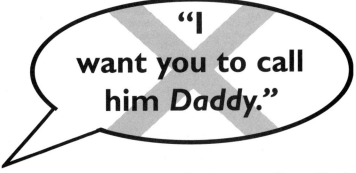

"I want you to call him *Daddy*."

Don't expect your stepchildren to call you Dad. And don't assume your children will want to address your new wife as Mommy or Mother. Let the stepchildren decide what they want to call you. Allow your children input on what name to use for their stepmother. The children's comfort level is most important here.

If the children don't settle on a name naturally, meet with them to establish a name that you're mutually comfortable with. "What would be a good name to call her?" is an appropriate piece of Parent Talk to open a meeting between you and your children about how to address their stepmother. This inquiry indicates your desire to be respectful of your children's wishes and empowers them by giving them some control over an issue that is important to them. It shows them that you honor their need to create a name they can be comfortable with.

Let your stepchildren know right away that you and your new spouse have established a unified parenting approach.

"We talked about it together and decided together."

"This is how we're both going to handle this situation."

"Both of us are in agreement on this."

Parenting children is tough enough when parents disagree on important discipline, financial, and spiritual issues. Raising other people's children is a special challenge, one that requires a united front presented by both the adults to all the children.

Correcting your own children requires skill and an open heart. Correcting your spouse's children requires skill, an open heart, and the full support of your partner.

Hopefully, the how-do-we-discipline-children dialogue began long before you got remarried. If so, it's likely that you chose a partner who has parenting beliefs in line with your own. In that case it becomes easy to use the Parent Talk sentence "This is how we do it in our family" and mean it.

SCHOOL

We all want kids to do well in school. So we go to parent-teacher conferences, read school communications that come home, check homework, and examine report cards. We move to an area that has a reputation for having "good" schools, put our kids in a private school, or homeschool them. We arrange for tutors if necessary. Some of us begin a college fund the day our child is born.

We give our children a pep talk before the school year begins and ask them, "How is school going?" almost every day. We call the teacher if a problem occurs, or someone calls us. We work together with the professional educators as much as possible. Some of us request a special teacher or ask that our child be removed from a classroom if we think it's in their best interest.

But are we doing enough to make sure our kids receive a good education? Are we perhaps overlooking some of the small, everyday stuff that could make a difference in their school lives?

In this section you will learn that your Parent Talk concerning education, study time, and school assignments is critical. It can help or hinder your child's view of education and of themselves. It can motivate or discourage, inspire or wound.

There is no quick fix to get your children to love and enjoy school. There is no one piece of Parent Talk you can use that will magically transform an unmotivated student into a motivated one. There is no magic that will help your child move his reading level up four years in six months. There is only a series of verbal and structural strategies that need to be implemented and used consistently throughout the school year. These skills will work if you choose to work the skills. Your child didn't learn to be unmotivated, dislike school, or be silent about conveying school information overnight, and she won't learn to change any of that overnight either.

Invest the time in learning to use the Parent Talk in this section to encourage, motivate, and inspire. You, your child, and your child's education are worth it.

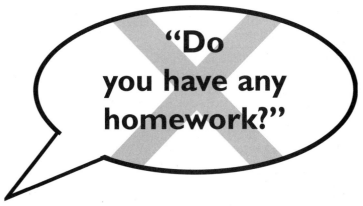

"Do you have any homework?"

Who do you think mentions homework first in families, the children or the parent? If you said "the parent," you're right. Parents bring up the subject of homework much more often than children do. And parents often ask, "Do you have any homework?" within the first five minutes of greeting their children after school.

Mentioning homework shortly after he arrives home from school tells your son that how much homework he has is more important to you than he is. Having not seen him all day, it might be helpful to ask a question or use Parent Talk that is more supportive and connecting. Perhaps your initial comment could be one that focuses on welcoming and maintaining relationship.

"I hope you created a happy day today."

"Hey, I'm glad you're here. There's a snack on the table. Feel free to help yourself."

"Welcome home. Hope things went well for you today."

"I'm glad you were here when I got home. I'm always glad to see you."

Bringing up homework before your child does is a signal that you care more about the homework than he does. It's one sign that you might be over-functioning. When you care more than your child does, there is less room for him to care. Someone else is already assuming the caring role. And that person is you.

If you take responsibility for mentioning homework, the child doesn't have to. It's not his job. It's yours. Your children will not step up and assume responsibility for homework unless the person who is currently handling that responsibility steps down. Step down and give them room to step up. Ideas for how to do that follow.

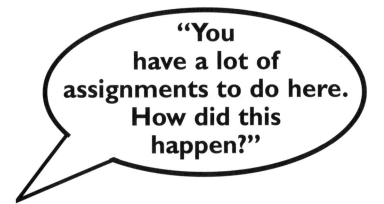

"You have a lot of assignments to do here. How did this happen?"

It's important to ascertain if your child's homework is the result of him not doing the work in class or of all students getting assigned homework on top of the work they did in school. Homework that is assigned to everyone can be completed in the family study time as outlined in the pages that follow.

Not doing school work in the time provided at school calls for a meeting with the teacher. More information is needed here than your child is likely to supply. It's important to hear from the teacher what behaviors your child is engaging in to avoid doing school work during school hours and what steps the teacher has taken to encourage different behaviors from him.

Wasting time in school is a classroom management issue and is best handled in the classroom while it's happening. Expecting you to handle school situations at home is an invasion of family time and a shirking of personal responsibility on the part of the teacher and the child. Expecting you to

"I DON'T KNOW WHY YOU'RE SO MAD. IT JUST PROVES YOU WERE RIGHT ABOUT THE TV TURNING MY BRAINS TO MUSH."

have the child do work at night that he was supposed to complete in school is an intrusion on family time and needs to be discouraged.

On the other hand, uncompleted assignments may result in your child falling behind on basic skills that will be necessary in order for him to master more complex concepts later on. In those cases, we recommend giving him a choice. "You can choose to complete your work at school or you can choose to do it on Saturday. You can decide." Call the teacher on Friday to see what incomplete work is essential and follow through by allowing your child to experience the consequences of his actions. Another role you can play here is to help him create a plan to finish schoolwork at school.

Solution seeking, brainstorming, creating a plan and following through are skills children can use their entire lives. You can help them practice those skills in situations such as this.

"It's homework time."

Misty's parents believe in encouraging her to do well in school. They attend parent-teacher conferences, show interest in her papers and report cards, and do their best to help her if she gets stuck with homework. They even have a special time, between seven and eight p.m., that is set aside as *homework time.*

Each evening, as seven p.m. arrives, Misty's dad announces, "It's homework time," and begins what all too often erupts into a full-blown argument. A typical conversation follows:

"It's homework time."

"I don't have any homework. I did it all at school."

"You always have homework."

"Not always and not tonight. I don't have any."

"Let me see your math book and what you did in class."

"I left it in my locker because I had it finished."

"What about English? Don't you have a paper that's due next week?"

"It's almost done. I can finish it in one evening and I have more than a week to do it. I've got it covered."

"Are you sure you don't have homework? What about history? Did you get that all done?"

"Yes, I got my history done. The teacher gave us time to read it in class. Don't you believe me?"

"I have a tough time believing you don't have any homework since I was surprised to hear about so many incomplete assignments at parent-teacher conferences last month."

"Well, I don't have any."

Such hassles over *homework time* could be significantly reduced with a slight adjustment in the Parent Talk used. Change the words and the concept of *homework time* to *feed-your-brain time.*

"It's feed-your-brain time."

Feed-your-brain time is family time where **everyone** does something that feeds their brain. You already have a feed-your-body time. It's called dinner. Perhaps the feed-your-brain time could follow the feed-your-body time. We eat together and then we feed our brains together.

"It's homework time" creates the impression that the time allotted is for homework only. When that routine has been established, it's a natural step for children to assume that if they have no homework they're free to fill that time slot with whatever other activities they feel like doing.

"It's *feed-your-brain time*" announces that this is an opportunity to grow our brains. It communicates the importance of growing our brains by feeding it healthy nutrients.

As everyone gathers for feed-your-brain time, each person can go in turn and tell what he or she is going to do with their time. Most children who have homework will choose to do it at this time. Although feed-your-brain time is often used for school-related activities such as doing homework, reviewing, studying, or reading for further information, it is not used exclusively for that purpose. This family time can be used to play vocabulary games, read educational articles, research topics of interest, practice a foreign language, or anything else that feeds the brain healthy material.

We are suggesting you can reduce schoolwork confrontation in your family by changing your Parent Talk and the notion of *homework time* to *feed-your-brain time*. When your Parent Talk becomes, "It's feed-your-brain time," the response, "I don't have any homework," takes on new meaning. A child doesn't need homework to engage in feeding his or her brain. Hence, arguing, questioning, and defending around the issue of homework are reduced significantly.

We want to be really clear about this. Feed-your-brain time is *family time*. That means everyone in the family is feeding their brain. Yes, it is important that each adult does something to feed their brains during this period, too. Do you really expect your children to do healthy things that you don't model? If you expect them to sit at the kitchen table and feed their brains while you watch your favorite TV show, you have unrealistic expectations. This is a family commitment to healthy living. If you aren't willing to make this commitment, then don't ask your children to do it either.

Refrain from giving unsolicited help during feed-your-brain time. Help that is not asked for is resented and is often not even needed. Give your child the space to ask for help if he needs it. Learning to ask for help is an important skill that every child needs to learn. So is struggling on your own for a while.

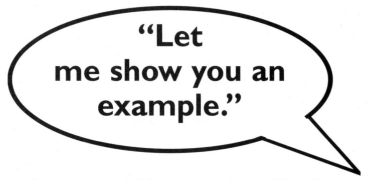

Sometimes children want help. The danger involved in helping is that helping doesn't always help. It can lead to learned helplessness.

Giving an example focuses on teaching, not doing it for them. Doing it for them is overfunctioning. Instead, show your child a sample, example, or possibility. Allow her to decide how to apply your contribution. Let her do the problems she was assigned.

Sometimes children want your checking help. Sometimes they don't. Let them make this decision initially.

Checking without permission sends the silent

message that you don't believe in your child's ability to complete the task by himself. It communicates, "I don't trust you to do this alone."

If you get data from a teacher that reveals your child could use some checking help, create a plan with him to allow that to happen. Practice doesn't make perfect. Practice makes permanent. It doesn't help your son to have him practicing a skill incorrectly. Nor does it help him for you to check up on him after he has mastered the skill. Together you can create the necessary balance of independence and assistance.

How about checking the first few examples and then turn him loose if he shows mastery? Or create a mutual plan to have you check every fourth problem, every third question, or every other example? Work it out together so he has control over how much checking help he receives.

Children will often tell you, "I don't know how to do it." Resist showing them right away. They're doing their I-can't act. Know that it is an act. Encourage them to choose a different act by saying,

"Act as if you can."

Other ways to send the same message include:

"Pretend that you know how."

"Play as if you know."

"If you did know how to begin, how would you begin?"

"If you did know what to write, what would you write?"

"If you did know how to spell it, how would you spell it?"

"Act as if you've done this five times already."

"Pretend that you're a pro at this."

Asking children to "act as if" doesn't mean they will do it correctly. It gets them started. It gets them doing something.   You can correct incorrect doing. Not doing anything is impossible to correct.

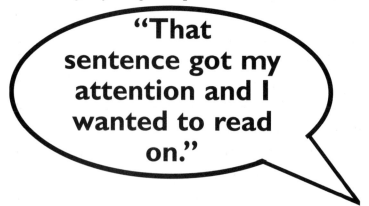

"The two facts you put in here really helped me understand the point you were making."

"You remembered to indent every paragraph."

"I can read every word."

"You got sixteen out of eighteen on the first attempt."

"You remembered that from last night."

"You stayed right on it and finished that section in ten minutes."

The comments above are examples of descriptive praise. They are samples of Parent Talk we recommend you use to replace evaluative comments such as "Good job" or "Excellent paper." Evaluative praise is global in nature and not specific enough to give the child useful information. This type of praise does little to teach why the effort was good or excellent. Evaluative praise using adjectives such as good, excellent, fantastic, super, superb, awesome, beautiful, tremendous, or wonderful only rates, judges, or evaluates. It does not teach.

Children do not need evaluation. They need affirmation. Descriptive praise describes and affirms children for what they have done, created, or demonstrated. These factual statements affirm while simultaneously giving valuable information the child can use now or later.

Another benefit of speaking with descriptive praise is that it allows the child to make the evaluation. You say, "You remembered to indent every paragraph," and your son says to himself, "I did a good job." You say, "You stayed right on it and finished that section in ten minutes," and your daughter thinks internally, "I was focused and fast." In each case the evaluation comes from the inside out rather than trying to fill the child up with evaluations from the outside in.

"You sure are smart."

"You really showed your brains there."

"You are one intelligent person."

Parents who praise their children's intelligence think they're building confidence by helping them create accurate pictures of their abilities. The parents assume that with this perception of themselves as intelligent, the children will be less likely to underperform. It doesn't work that way.

Believing that you're intelligent doesn't always translate into high performance. In fact, sometimes the opposite occurs. Kids who have been taught to believe they're smart will often give up quickly on things they don't think they're good at. They're afraid a failure might show that they're not intelligent after all. So they choose risk avoidance as a strategy to maintain their view of themselves as intelligent.

Praise effort over intelligence. Just because you have a high intelligence quotient (IQ) or believe that you're smart doesn't mean you don't have to engage in effort. Overrating intelligence and underrating the importance of effort does not help a child become internally motivated to achieve.

"You worked on that for over an hour."

"It took you four drafts, but you stuck with it. You nailed it."

"You must have worked really hard."

Praising effort gives children a variable over which they have some control. They cannot control their intelligence, but they can control their effort. Using Parent Talk that praises effort helps children develop their sense of personal power. They learn to see themselves as in control of their level of success.

When children learn that intelligence is the key to success, they come to believe that effort is not important. They then rationalize that giving effort means their innate intelligence was not enough. Not wanting to appear unintelligent, they make minimal effort.

"It's time for a time-out."

Frustration may occur during feed-the-brain time. One of the reasons why it's important to have you there feeding your own brain is so you can keep track of the frustration level. Suggest that your child take a time-out if you see her becoming over-stressed.

Go shoot some baskets, ride bikes, go for a walk. Get away from the brainwork for a while whether it's school related or not. When she comes back to the task, she will bring a fresh mind and a fresh attitude.

"Feed-your-brain time is over."

Pushing beyond the set brain-feeding time creates diminished results. Set a limit and stick to it. Hold to the set time schedule.

Do not let your children do schoolwork for long periods of time. Family time is MORE important than spending hours working on school assignments. If the teachers assign more than is doable in the feed-your-brain time you have structured (ninety minutes for high school, sixty minutes for middle school, thirty minutes for elementary school), call the teachers and let them know they're assigning too much material.

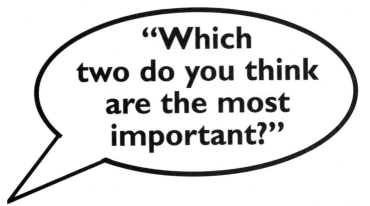

"**Which two do you think are the most important?**"

When there appears to be more school work assigned than there is time necessary to complete it, ask your daughter, "Which two of your assignments do you think are most important?" This type of question requires her to think and to set priorities, helping her learn a valuable life skill in the process.

"Which assignment would be best to finish?" asks her to make an evaluation. "Put your assignments in order of importance" requires her to do an appraisal and rank the order from most to least. You are asking her to think, make a judgment, form an opinion and follow through. These activities are often more valuable than the one the teacher assigned.

Invest some time inviting your child to use her brain for thinking.

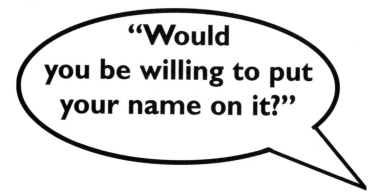

This Parent Talk phrase is not used to check on whether your children remembered to put their name on the paper as most teachers require. Rather, it's a statement about the relationship between pride and effort. "Would you be willing to put your name on it?" really means, "Are you proud enough of it to sign it?" Help your children learn to develop an internal standard of excellence so they know how this piece of work stacks up against their personal standard.

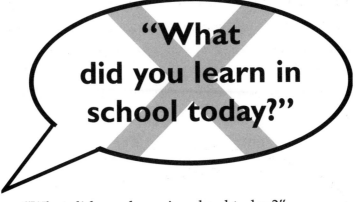

"What did you learn in school today?"
"Nothing."
"Anything interesting happen?"
"Nope."
"Did you enjoy school today?"
"It was OK."

Does getting your kids to offer information about school seem more difficult than pulling teeth? Do you ever feel like a lawyer cross-examining them in an attempt to find out what's really happening at school? Do you wish they would volunteer more information about their educational experience so you wouldn't have to ask so often? If so, read on.

Ask questions that require more than a one-word response. "Did you have a good day today?" and "How did it go today?" require only one-word answers. If you ask that kind of question, you do not encourage a lengthy response. The child can answer "Yes" and "Fine." Instead, ask a question that requires some thought. "Tell me about the most interesting thing that happened to you today" and "What surprised you about school today?" will often generate more lengthy responses.

Children don't enjoy playing twenty questions. When you see them at the end of the school day, limit your questions. Rotate them so you create some variety. No one enjoys being asked the same question every day. Asking twenty questions in one day or the same few questions every day feels like prying. Children resist prying by clamming up.

If your child begins to tell you about school or even offers only a one-word response, "Say some more" will often elicit further information. "Say some more" is a gentle invitation that encourages the child to keep talking. It doesn't come across as probing, as a direct question might. "Please continue," "Go on," and "Keep going" are Parent Talk phrases that politely suggest to him that it's still his turn and you'd like to hear more. They tell him you're still in the listening stance and don't want to control the direction of the conversation. They leave him at choice over what and how much to share.

When you take control of the direction of the after-school discussion, you come across as desper-

"WANNA TALK ABOUT YOUR DAY?"

ate. Children can smell desperation and often use it to their advantage. "I want to know what happened on your English test" is Parent Talk that puts you in control and invites resistance. When you come across as desperately wanting information, you encourage the child to cling to whatever it is he has that seems so valuable to you. It gives him a sense of power to withhold from an adult something the adult appears to want so badly.

If your child does talk about school, stop talking and assume the listening stance. Give him the space to talk. Listen nonjudgmentally. Nothing will stop the flow of information faster than judging what is said. When you react like a judge, the information flow dries up.

Don't expect that your child is going to tell you everything that goes on at school. It's not going to happen. Be active and involved. Find out what's going on by being present. Get involved at school. Talk to the teachers regularly.

Also use your parenting network to glean school information. If you don't have a *what's going on at school* network, get one. Rely on the other parents in your child's classroom to provide you with information. Remember that, in a network, information flows both ways. So when you have useful information or hear a disturbing report, contact the parents in your network. See what they know and share what you have learned.

"**We have to have a talk about this report card.**"

If you waited to talk to your child about the importance of school and grades until after she received her report card, you waited too long. A conversation about grades and report cards needs to happen early and often. Expectations about grades, what they mean, the value you place on them, and their importance to you and your child can be discussed from the beginning of her school experience.

When you do discuss a report card with your child, listen more than talk. Ask lots of questions, not from an interrogation stance, but rather from a desire to get her involved in sharing her opinion. Ask her:

"How do you feel about these grades? What do you attribute them to?"

"Were there any surprises on this report card for you?"

" What are you most proud of?"

"Are there any disappointments here for you?"

"What is one goal you have for the next reporting period?"

"I'M AFRAID THERE'S GOING TO BE A LOT OF DISCUSSION BETWEEN 'HERE'S MY REPORT CARD' AND 'WHERE DO I SIGN?'"

Use Parent Talk that focuses on learning about the child's report card from her point of view before sharing your own.

When reacting to a report card, allow your Parent Talk to be descriptive rather than evaluative. Evaluative responses like "good job," "excellent," "superb," "lousy," "pitiful," and "poor" are not helpful. Evaluation does not teach or give the child useful information. Describe what you see, and leave the evaluation for the child. "Looks like you're a bit down from last time." "Two teachers mentioned missing assignments."

Children who receive a positive report card need affirmation, not evaluation. Affirm what they have accomplished with descriptive comments. "I notice your grade went up in two classes." "Every one of your teachers said they enjoyed having you in class."

Report cards come home several times a year. You will have more than one opportunity to use these ideas with your children. When you do, keep in mind that your relationship with them is more important than anything written on their report card.

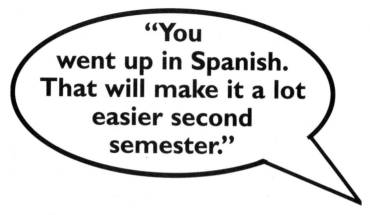

"You went up in Spanish. That will make it a lot easier second semester."

When discussing information on the child's report card, allow your Parent Talk to tie the information on the card to possible effects.

"You went up in Spanish." (Information from the report card.) "That will make it a lot easier second semester." (Effect of the information on the report card.)

"Your math grade dropped some." (Information from the report card.) "That leaves you behind in the basics." (Effect of the information on the report card.)

"Your teacher says you socialize a lot in class." (Information from the report card.) "That's got to make it hard to concentrate on the information being presented." (Effect of the information on the report card.)

Helping children make the connection between cause and effect is an ongoing responsibility of parents. Use this report card opportunity to help your children see the possible effects (outcomes), both positive and negative, of the results they produced in school.

When communicating negative feelings about school work, use Parent Talk that separates the deed from the doer. "I love you and I'm not real happy about this report card" helps the child see that it's the results you don't enjoy, not the person.

Likewise, stay away from comments such as, "I love you so much when you bring home a report card like this." This style of communication obviously tells the child that your love is linked to high grades and implies that if the grades go down so will your love.

> **"Grades are important, and who you are is made up of a lot more than what is on this report card."**

Yes, grades are important. They are a measure of the skills your child has developed and the concepts he or she has mastered regarding what this particular group of school personnel feels is important. Grades can be a ticket to a certain college or the signal that sends your child onto a specific career path. They can also be an indication of the effort he brings to the school situation.

Discussion about the value you place on grades, school work, and learning needs to be communicated repeatedly throughout your children;s school years. Another communication that needs to be made regularly is that they are not their grades. Grades are only a partial reflection of who and what they really are, know, and are capable of becoming. Grades measure only what their particular school defines as intelligent. That narrow definition of intelligence does not measure emotional intelligence, spontaneity, integrity, trustworthiness, fortitude, sensitivity, creativity, and a host of other important characteristics.

When discussing the importance of learning and this particular report card, keep in mind that school is simply the water your children are splashing around in. Although they are enrolled in classes called geometry, literature, art, music, social studies, and government, what they are really doing is learning how to swim. They are learning the skills necessary to swim through life successfully.

Your children are learning how to . . .

- act with confidence.
- overcome obstacles.
- deal with all kinds of teachers and classmates.
- respect diversity.
- develop interpersonal skills.
- achieve personal goals.
- persevere.
- prioritize.
- think critically.
- think for themselves.
- develop an internal standard of excellence and behavior.
- develop their sense of personal power.
- believe in themselves.
- develop self-responsibility.
- become motivated from within.
- respect the ideas and opinions of others.

- disagree politely.
- work cooperatively.
- work independently.
- demonstrate self-discipline.
- own their behavioral choices.
- make amends.

A report card is only one measure of success at school. Don't treat it as the be-all and end-all of information about what your children are learning or who they are as human beings. Again, your child is not his or her grades. Communicate about report cards with that in mind.

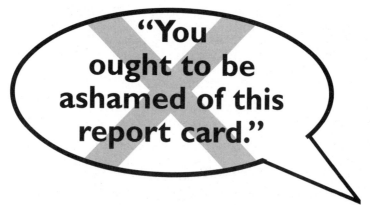

"You ought to be ashamed of this report card."

"You ought to be ashamed of yourself," Larry Johnson said to his ten-year-old daughter after looking over her report card. "You haven't taken school work seriously. All you do is lie around watching television, playing video games, and talking to your friends on your cell phone. Your poor mother tries to help you, but all you do is blow her off. Don't you have any respect or level of feeling for your mother or pride in yourself? If you do, you don't show it. Do you see her gray hairs? Where do you suppose those came from? You're going to be the death of her the way you ignore her efforts. She loves you so much and you treat her like she's invisible. I hope you're proud of yourself, because I'm not. I expect to see a radical change in your behavior starting right now. Go over and give your mother a hug and tell her you'll do better in school from now on. Go on, do it now."

Larry Johnson did what a lot of parents do to manipulate their children into behaving in a desired fashion or achieving a desired result. He dispensed a huge dose of guilt.

Parents who use shame and guilt as a motivator for grades or to achieve any other goal do so because they believe the technique is needed to encourage children to change. They dispense verbal abuse because they believe that if children can be shamed into feeling guilty they will change their behavior and do what their parents want.

There are times when shaming works and produces the behavior we want from our children. But at what price? Children who are shamed regularly come to believe that the shame is justified, that they must have earned it, and that they deserve it. They develop core beliefs such as "I'm no good," "I'm not enough," "I'm wrong," and "I'm not worthwhile."

Children who have these core beliefs see themselves as shameful and act in accordance with their beliefs.

This negative belief system tends to attract increased shaming from the significant adults in their lives, which reinforces their negative core beliefs. These children often get caught up in a self-deprecating cycle of behaviors that elicit negative parental responses—a cycle that is difficult to exit.

Shame and guilt often backfire. Their use produces resistance and resentment. Children realize on some level they are being manipulated, pushed, and controlled by Parent Talk that shames. Control is resented. Manipulation breeds resentment. Pushing calls forth pushing back.

Parents who use shame in an effort to dispense guilt don't always do it as blatantly as Larry Johnson did with his daughter. Parents often do guilt tripping so subtly that they're unaware their behavior is shame based. If you're using any of the following Parent Talk phrases with your children, you are injecting shame into your language patterns.

"You ought to be ashamed of yourself."

"That report card makes me feel bad."

"What will your grandmother think?"

"I'm glad your dead grandfather isn't here to see this."

"I can't sleep at night worrying about you."

"Someone who loves their mother [father] would

never do that."

"Jesus wouldn't like that."

"You should know better."

"And you call yourself a Christian [Mormon, Jew, Muslim, Methodist, Baptist, etc.]."

"Your behavior gives me headaches."

"God sees everything you do."

If you hear yourself using any of these sentences, or others like them, consider an alternative approach. Instead of shamebased communications, use Parent Talk that is open, honest, and direct. Present choices to your children. Explain what happens if they choose a certain behavior and what happens if they don't. Allow them to choose and then experience the legitimate consequences of their behavior. If you have strong feelings about a report card or behavior, tell the child directly. Explain the reasons for your feelings. Step out of the resistance-resentment cycle by telling children exactly what you expect and why.

"I'm angry about this report card and you will need to create a plan to bring these grades up" is more effective than "You should have known better." "Looks like you've chosen to work with a tutor this marking period. The two D's demonstrate that you can use some extra time and help in those subjects" is healthier than the guilt-laying, "You really disappointed us with this report card."

Children learn more from a caring adult who

helps them to evaluate their choices and the results that follow than they do from one who shames and continually dispenses guilt. Refuse to be one of those parents who cause children to feel shame and guilt for their actions. Communicate honestly without sneaking shame into the equation. Whether talking about schoolwork or any other issue, stay centered in your efforts to create respectful, responsible children by modeling positive attributes in your behavior and in your Parent Talk.

Punishments don't work. Consequences and natural outcomes do. What are the natural consequences of poor grades? Having a tutor work with you on Saturday mornings is one. Going to a learning specialist three days a week after school is another. Investing part of your summer retaking a class is a third.

Keep the consequences imposed for poor schoolwork similar to those in other areas of your children's lives. They need to be reasonable, related, and respectful.

Being grounded for a month is not reasonable. Giving up your Saturdays until you get caught up on your schoolwork is.

Not being able to ride your bike is not related. Going to a learning specialist three days a week is.

Getting angry and exploding in a brief rage is not respectful. Explaining to your child that "opportunity equals responsibility" does show respect. It also helps him see the connection between cause and effect. "When the responsibility remains strong (a satisfactory report card), so does the opportunity to choose your own activities on Saturday mornings. When the responsibility drops, so does the opportunity to structure your own Saturday morning."

Surprise Talk

One of the best things you can do for your children in regard to school, learning, and grades is to expect their success and communicate that expectation to them. Hold positive expectations for them and verbalize that mental posture often.

Use surprise talk when presented with a negative report card. "Wow. This is surprising" and "I never expected this" are ways to communicate that you hold higher expectations of your child than her report card reflects. "I'm not surprised" communicates that you expect poor performance in school matters.

When she brings home a positive report card, use surprise talk in a different way. "Knowing you the way I do, this type of report doesn't surprise me." This style of Parent Talk lets your child know exactly what you expect in terms of school performance.

Adding a reason to your lack of surprise strengthens your communication by helping your child connect the dots. "This doesn't surprise me. Not after the way I've seen you study and prepare for tests. Congratulations."

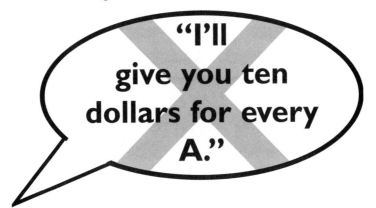

Rewards are ineffective if developing a love of learning in your child is your goal. Paying kids ten dollars for each A, treating them to ice cream if they bring home a good report card, or buying a new video game if they get on the honor role promotes only short-term results at best. What attaching rewards to grades really teaches children is that you don't study so you can learn and grow, you study so you can get a treat or special concert tickets.

Paying children for grades or attaching any other incentive teaches them that learning is not the goal, nor is it even the grade itself. The real goal is ice cream, a new laptop, or adding text messaging to their phone. Love of learning is swallowed up and obstructed by focusing on the pursuit of material goods.

Paying you fifty dollars for every strategy you implement from this book does little to help you learn about the importance of becoming a skillful parent. It might entice you to care in the short term. But if we withdraw the pay, you will likely withdraw your interest and attention.

"What are the possibilities for improving in algebra?"

"What can you do about this?"

"Do you have a plan?"

"Where do you want to go from here?"

Focus on solution seeking. Talking and thinking about what you have defined as a problem brings negative energy to the situation and keeps you stuck in what is. Turning your attention to solution seeking infuses the discussion with positive energy and helps you concentrate on moving things forward to a different ending. Fix the problem rather than fixing blame by searching for solutions.

"What is your goal?"

"What is your goal for next marking period?"

"What kind of comments would you like to see on your report card?"

"Exactly how much do you want to improve in Literature?"

Goals provide direction. They also serve as benchmarks so your children can tell where they are in the process of achieving a goal. Your job as a parent is to help your children set realistic goals—ones they have a 70 or 80 percent chance of achieving. If the goal is unattainable, they will get discouraged easily. If the goal is too low, there is minimal satisfaction gained from reaching it.

Once your child has set an academic goal, help him learn that he cannot "do" a goal. He can only do activities that will help him move closer to his goal.

Example:

If his goal is to stay current in history class, there are specific activities he can do that will help him move closer to achieving that goal.

1. Write each assignment in my responsibility notebook the moment it's assigned.
2. Check my backpack every day to see that I turned everything in.
3. Check with the teacher every Friday to see if all assignments are in.
4. Do any missing assignments on Saturday.

Creating a goal and listing possible activities to reach that goal helps children create a picture in their minds of how to achieve that goal, keep track of how they're doing, and celebrate small successes along the way.

"There's no such thing as a permanent record."

Some school personnel are fond of telling students, "This is going to go in your permanent record." They use the permanent record reference as a threat to get students to comply with the adult mandates and to care about school.

In reality, there is no such thing as a permanent record. Tell your children the truth:

"Every day is a new day."

"You can always start over."

"You can set a new course today."

Yes, children occasionally make poor choices and need to make amends. Yes, some people are slow to forgive, and a reputation can stick in their minds. True, the report card was done in ink. Those grades are not changeable, and they can be improved.

What is, is. You cannot change these grades. They are what they are. It is where the child goes from here, what she does with the information that is on the report card, that is important. The next step is the only one that can be taken now.

There is no such thing as a permanent record.

"A new adventure is coming."

Latrell was moving from Head Start to kindergarten. Ho Lin was moving from one day care center to another. Kevin was moving across town. Although their situations were different, each youngster was in need of a parent who could respond effectively to the pending transition.

Your job as a parent during any transition is to create and structure conditions conducive to producing readiness for a smooth transition. It takes time for a child to get used to and embrace a new situation. It takes time for a parent to tune into and respond effectively to a child's positive and negative reactions to the change.

Be honest and open with your children, keeping them informed of your plans as they develop.

"We're considering a move to a new city."

"Moving into ninth grade will require experiencing a new school."

"Mrs. Wilson will not be at day care after this week."

A minor transition for you can be a big deal for your child. Remember, to a four-year-old, the last two years represent half of her life. Give children real reasons why the transitions are necessary.

"We're considering the move because it's a promotion at the office."

"Ninth grade means being in the high school with mostly older students."

"Mrs. Wilson has decided to start her family and is pregnant."

"**We're going to see how the new school works.**"

Arrange for a visitation at the new school. Set it up as if you're checking it out, looking it over.

"Let's go over and see what that school looks like."

"I'd like to see the classrooms and the playground."

Treat this as an exploration, an adventure into discovery. Give your child and yourself some things to look for.

"Let's see if we can find how this school is the same/different than the last school."

"Let's find out what you like and don't like about it."

"Maybe we can come up with some questions we'd like to have answered."

Debrief the visitation. After it's over, ask your child what she saw that looked fun and what she heard that sounded interesting. "What surprised you?" is a question that often produces helpful dialogue. "Did you see anything exciting or scary?" is another. Your goal here is to get the child talking.

Your job during the debriefing is to give her an opportunity to describe what she heard, saw, and felt. Concentrate on getting information, not on giving information. As your child talks about her experience she will move through it and free herself from places where she could get stuck.

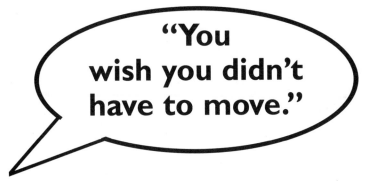

"You wish you didn't have to move."

Demonstrate understanding by granting in fantasy what you cannot grant in reality. Children faced with a big transition will often remark, "I like my old school better" or "I don't want a new teacher." In these situations it's not helpful to attempt reassurance with comments such as, "You'll get used to it in time," or "Just give it a chance. You'll probably end up liking it better."

More helpful than reassurance is Parent Talk that demonstrates your understanding of your child's experience by recognizing and honoring her wish. "You wish you could stay with Miss Sally forever" shows empathy and understanding while helping your child feel heard. "You'd like it best if you could pick your own teacher" tunes into the child's fantasy without communicating that the wish will be granted.

"I know you're up to it."

After demonstrating understanding by granting in fantasy what you cannot in reality, send your child a capability message. "I know you can handle it" or "I know you're up to it" are examples of Parent Talk that sends the silent message, "I see you as capable." "I know you can handle it" doesn't communicate that everything will be wonderful. It just lets your child know you believe he can handle whatever occurs.

"School will be starting up in a couple of weeks."

Create a positive attitude about going back to school. Talk to your children about being able to see their friends, meet their new teacher, and all the opportunities that being at school provides. Focus on their areas of interest and emphasize the ways in which school helps make it possible for them to pursue those interests. When your children speak negatively, acknowledge their concern and redirect them to positive thoughts.

"We're going to begin moving toward our regular school schedule."

Start the school schedule early. Break the summer sleep-in/stay-up-late mode. Don't just spring this on your children. Begin the morning and evening school routine at least two weeks before school actually starts. Announce that bedtime and wake-up time will be changed beginning on Monday. Slowly adjust the schedule over a two-week period until these times fall in line with the regular school-year schedule.

Don't expect that your children will be able to make the adjustment to getting up for school quickly or easily without a break-in period. Take the full two weeks to work into the routine slowly by adjusting the bedtime and wake-up time a few minutes every day until the desired time is reached.

Your goal is to have the schedule set prior to the first day of school.

MONEY TALK

Do you talk to your children about money? Yes, you do. Every parent does, whether they think they do or not.

Some parents talk to children about money with intentionality. They do it on purpose at the dinner table, in the car on the way to school, or at the store while shopping. Others do it unknowingly by talking in the presence of their children—on the phone, with relatives, walking in the mall. Whether you're aware of it or not, your children are hearing how you talk about money.

If you don't talk about money much in front of your children, they're hearing that, too. They are hearing that money is not safe to talk about, not a subject to ask questions about, a taboo topic. They hear about money whether words come out of your mouth or not.

You may or may not be experiencing money challenges right now. Regardless of your current financial situation, are you comfortable talking about money with your children? How effective are you at talking about money? What words do you use when you talk about money in front of or directly to your children?

If your money talk is infrequent, be aware that your children are developing their money consciousness from information they get from TV, peers, and what they pick up on the street. Most of that is inaccurate and incongruent with your family values. Use this section to take charge of your child's financial education and get it going in the direction you desire.

In this section we will explore some of the Parent Talk about money typically used with children. It will include phrases, sentences, and ways of speaking that will help your children become financially literate, self-responsible, and personally empowered in relation to money. Use it to improve your skill and confidence when talking to them about this important topic.

> **"It's allowance time. Everybody get your envelopes."**

Yes, we believe in allowances. An allowance is money that a child gets for being part of the family. It is *not* money he is paid in exchange for doing chores. The main purpose of a child's allowance is to help him learn how to spend, save, and use money effectively. A child needs some money in order to learn how to do that.

"I pay my child only when she does chores," a father recently told us. "No work, no pay. It's the

American way." Our beliefs about chores and money differ significantly from the beliefs of this father.

Chores are important in a family. Every family member has some. Chores are assigned or chosen based on age, ability, and interest. Even a toddler can take her dinner plate to the kitchen after eating. The reason for chores is *not* to earn money. Chores are necessary because completing chores is what it takes to help the family function smoothly and effectively. We all contribute to the family's well-being because we are all a part of the family. The important lesson for children to learn is that we do chores because we are part of a fully functioning family that cares about each other—not that you have to do chores to get money.

The envelope system is an organizational tool that will help you teach children about budgeting. Children are concrete thinkers. That means if it is not in their hands, it is not in their minds. Envelopes will help you make the dividing of money into different budgeting categories a concrete process.

Zipper bags work nicely because they have the added feature of being transparent. They're fun for children to use because they can actually see their money grow

Label the zipper bags or envelopes to designate several budget areas. We suggest these four:

- Savings (money to be used later)
- Spending (money to be used soon)
- Charity (money to be used to help others)
- Investment (money that will grow by itself)

Children can divide their own allowance by placing the amount of money they choose in the appropriate envelopes. With small children, you may want to decide how much money goes into each envelope. With older children, some mutually negotiated minimums may be necessary at first to begin the process. They can hold the money and the envelopes in their own hands as they divide their money into the concrete piles that the envelopes represent. As they see money, touch it, and divide it, budgeting becomes a real experience for them.

The main goal here is to teach your children a money routine, one that will help them develop money discipline that will last a lifetime. Be careful not to alter the procedure, make exceptions, or skip a week. The idea that's important to get across to them is that there is a system at work. If you work the system, the system works.

The root word of allowance is "allow." Allow your children the opportunity to learn about saving, charity, investing, and budgeting by announcing, "It's allowance time. Everyone get your envelopes."

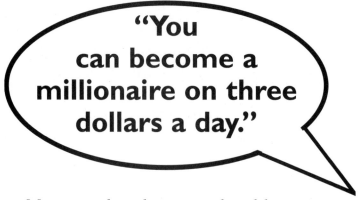

> "You can become a millionaire on three dollars a day."

Many people today are enslaved by consumer debt. They have many possessions and huge debts to go with them. Yet, they have little savings. To prevent your children from joining those ranks, teach them to invest.

Yes, you can be a millionaire by retirement age by investing three dollars a day. Setting aside money for school, a home, or retirement is a habit that can be started at an early age. So can the habit of indiscriminate spending.

Young adults, out on their own, can quickly amass debt by attempting to live the same lifestyle they enjoyed under their parents' roof. The money lessons you model and verbalize when they are young can help them build sound money practices long before they leave the nest.

Are you teaching your children to become a millionaire on three dollars a day, or to spend their millions one dollar, one cell phone, one CD, one video, and one pair of jeans at a time?

"I'll give you a little extra this time. You can owe it to me."

"My allowance is all gone and I need some gas money."

"Will you loan me some money until allowance day?"

"Can I have some extra money this week? I want a new set of Legos real bad and it will take me two weeks to save up enough to get it."

Credit alert! Credit alert!

Be aware that when you say, "You can owe it to me," you have just become your child's first credit card and lending institution. You have begun the process of instilling in him the feeling that he can get whatever he wants whenever he wants it, regardless of whether he has the money to do it or not. You have said yes to creating a belief system that claims you can have it now and pay for it later.

Do you really want to begin the credit card habit at this age? Or would you rather help your child experience and appreciate the value of paying cash? Buy now and pay later, or wait until you can afford

"WELL, IF YOU DON'T HAVE ANY MONEY, CAN WE GO TO THE ATM?"

to pay cash. Which habit do you want him to develop?

You get to say no if your child wants a loan. One way to do that is to use the Parent Talk phrase that follows.

"That's too bad. Sounds like you have a money problem. What can you do about it?"

When your child runs out of money and wants a loan, lead with empathy. "Bummer," "Darn, that's too bad," "What a shame" are examples of Parent Talk that begin with empathy. Communicated with sincerity, the empathy lead-in will discourage you from scolding with unhelpful Parent Talk such as, "I told you so, but you didn't listen to me," or "I warned you, and you did it again, huh?"

Follow your empathetic statement with "Sounds like you have a money problem." This statement serves two purposes. First, it communicates to the child that the current money problem he faces is *his* problem.

Second, and just as important, it reminds YOU that this is not YOUR problem. There are times when allowing children to experience the consequences of their actions and choices is the best way for them to learn. This in one of those times.

Remembering that this is not your problem helps you resist the urge to rescue. While we're unsure if bailing out car companies or savings and loan organizations is helpful or unhelpful to a global economy, we're certain that bailing out our children is NOT helpful. It teaches them they do not have to be responsible with their money because someone will always be there to give them more, pay their way, rescue them. This is not a healthy belief system for them to adopt.

Spending their discretionary money early and not having enough to get through the week is a valuable lesson for children. It teaches them to keep track of their money more closely, spend it wisely, and do without if they have none. It helps them learn about cause and effect and how the choices they make with their money produce specific results.

Asking the question, "What can you do about it?", points the child in the direction of solution seeking. At this time it would be helpful to cooperatively brainstorm other ways to generate income. Brainstorming helps children develop the skill of possibility thinking. It expands their vision by inviting them to see beyond simplistic yes and no responses or asking you for extra money. In addition, this stance places you in the role of supportive listener and helper without slipping into being the one who rescues or denies.

"I'm willing to pay part of it" is a phrase that is useful here. Use it when your child wants something that exceeds the amount you had earmarked in your budget. If you had eighty dollars set aside for a winter jacket and your daughter wants one that costs over a hundred dollars, using this sentence defines your limit. It also invites her to take responsibility for coming up with the difference. It curbs feelings of entitlement and allows her to take ownership for achieving what she wants. In addition, if some of her money is invested in the jacket she is more likely to take better care of it.

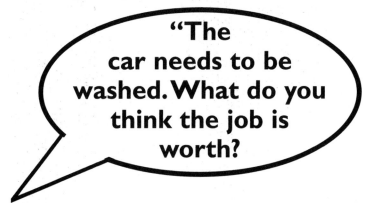

"The car needs to be washed. What do you think the job is worth?

"I need my shoes shined."

"The grass needs mowing."

"Do you want to take over one of my jobs? I have one I'd gladly pay to have someone do."

If your child feels she needs more money than

her allowance provides, there are additional ways to get it. Doing out of the ordinary jobs around the house over and above her normal chores is one way for her to earn additional income. This will help her internalize the concept that if she wants more she can work more.

"You won't have any money left."

"You'll be sorry if something unexpected comes up."

"You'll have to go the rest of the week without any money."

There may be a powerful lesson learned when children spend their money all at once. Do not protect them from experiencing the natural consequences of their choices. Allow these opportunities to happen and let the consequence do the teaching. When the consequence does the teaching, you are freed from that role and can concentrate on helping them debrief and search for solutions. It also keeps shame, ridicule, and "I told you so" from creeping into your Parent Talk.

Better to have your children learn the outcomes of spending all the money they have available at this time in their life, when the stakes are relatively small, than to learn it later as adults when the consequences are more costly.

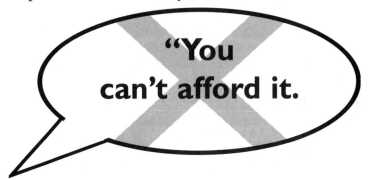

"That costs too much."

"You don't have enough money."

"It's way too expensive!"

These are verbal examples of well-meaning parents making money decisions for children. If you hear yourself uttering statements like these, be advised that you are doing your children's thinking for them. Why not allow them to do their own thinking?

Instead of deciding for them if something is too expensive, why not help them see how much it costs and guide them to compare that with how much money they have? Let them determine if they're willing to work to make up the difference. Give them the facts and the freedom to make financial decisions for themselves.

If not now, when?

Maybe and maybe not.

Even if you're correct in your assessment of the worth of the purchase from the point of view of monetary value, you might be missing the value inherent in the lesson learned from making the purchase. What if this "waste of money" ends up teaching an important lesson about making an impulse purchase, or about how to examine the quality of an item more accurately in the future? What if the purchase helps a child learn how to go without once he's spent all his funds? What if it gives him hours of practice in solution seeking as he attempts to put a broken item back together? What if it helps your child learn how to deal with disappointment?

Are those lessons a waste of money?

"That'll be a waste of your money" does one other thing. It tells your child, "I'm smart and you aren't. I'm big and you're little. I can make decisions and you can't." This style of Parent Talk leaves the child feeling little and stupid. It devalues his opinion and diminishes his sense of personal power. "That'll be a waste of your money" might save him some money. At the same time, it robs him of the value of an important life experience.

Remember that regardless of what your child says, those trendy clothes are not a necessity. She may want them badly, but they are not a need. There are only three basic needs in our lives. We need food, water, and love. If we don't have food or water, eventually we die. The same holds true for love, at least in our earliest years. If infants aren't stroked, cuddled, or loved, they die. Food, water, and love are needs. All the rest are wants.

Help your children understand the difference between need and want. They don't really need a new iPhone; they want one. They don't need gas money; they want it. They don't need another cookie; they want it.

"I need" is a way many children describe what they desire in their lives. "I need" is a whiny phrase. It signals dependency. "I need" has expectations

attached to it. When you announce "I need" something, the implication is that you expect someone to
fulfill that need for you. Since you expect your need
to be met, you assume a more passive stance and
aren't as likely to work to satisfy your desire yourself.

"I want" is a more self-sufficient expression. It
signals independence. It is simply a statement of
desire with no expectation attached to it. Because
you don't expect someone else to satisfy your
desire, you assume a more active stance and are
more likely to work toward fulfilling it.

Charlie's dad was a banker. Money *was* his job.
He told both his adolescent boys, "Don't ever worry
about money. That's my job. If you need any money,
come and ask me. I'll find a way to take care of it."
And he did take care of it. He took such good care
of the family money that neither son learned a
whole lot about it.

Both boys went off to college not knowing how

to balance a checkbook. Neither had ever written a check or seen a bill being paid. They had no knowledge of the family finances. They had no concept of how much electricity costs or what a car payment did to the family budget. Indeed, they had never seen a family budget.

This father, who spent his professional life in finance, raised two financially illiterate children. He set out to protect his children from money worries and ended up producing children ignorant of money matters.

We certainly don't want children worrying constantly about the family finances. We also don't want to keep them in the dark as to where money comes from and how it is spent in the family. Let your children in on the family budget and what it actually takes to provide for the family. Help them develop money knowledge and skills without creating undue worry.

"Here is where the money goes."

Kids don't often think about family bills. They may see cash come out of a purse to pay for groceries or a check handed to the music tutor. Yet most children know little about taxes, mortgages, or phone, gas, and electric bills. Very few parents invest the time to sit kids down and actually show them what it takes to support a family financially.

No, we are not suggesting that you create worry and anxiety over whether or not all the bills can be paid this month. We are, however, recommending that you help children develop an appreciation for where money goes and how much things cost.

How about a family meeting every other month where everyone sits at a table while bills are introduced and discussed? This is where children learn valuable life lessons that will help them become financially literate and independent.

They will learn:

- Some bills fluctuate each month, while others remain the same.
- Credit card companies charge you a lot of money if you don't pay them on time.
- Some bills come four times a year. Others come every month.
- Some bills are unexpected, like when the car died and had to be fixed.
- Insurance is important.
- The more channels you have on the TV, the more money it costs.
- It costs money to heat and cool the house.

Money information leads to money management. Money management leads to control of your money. Control of your money leads to financial security. Help your children start down that path today.

"Who wants to carry the grocery list?"

Take a list with you when you go grocery shopping. It will curb impulse buying and help you stick to your budget. It communicates to children that spending money involves a plan, and following that plan is important.

Valuable money lessons lurk in the grocery store aisles and can be used by the alert, unhurried parent. As you search for each item you can demonstrate and communicate comparative shopping principles. Compare for price and quantity. Discuss store brand vs. the advertised product. Are there sales that would warrant bulk buying? Do we have coupons? What does "per pound" and "per ounce" mean? If it all looks like hamburger, how come some costs more per pound?

It looks like a grocery store. Actually, it's a money school. You are the teacher. Enjoy the process of teaching and learning at the grocery school.

"Help me figure out the tip."

"Help me figure out the tip" is Parent Talk that helps children in several ways. Obviously, it provides a real-life opportunity to practice basic math skills. Helping children see and use situations that require doing math is practical and valuable. "Let's figure out the miles per gallon we got on this trip," "How much will we save if we use all these coupons?", and "How will the tax break the President is suggesting affect us?" are other possibilities.

"Help me figure out the tip" also gives children an awareness of the cost of the meal so they can appreciate what is being provided for them. Why keep them in the dark about the cost of sneakers, a new car, or the fee charged by the roofer?

Another benefit of learning about tipping is that it gives children the message that being appreciative for a service provided is often expressed in the form of a monetary tip. Tipping can occur with the person who carries your bags to the airline ticket counter, the babysitter, or the cab driver. In addition to figuring the tip, it's a valuable experience for children to physically handle the tip and be the one who expresses verbal as well as monetary appreciation as he or she presents it to the person who performed the service.

"Oh, I think you gave me the wrong change."

Allow your children to overhear you telling cashiers or waiters when the change is incorrect. If you were shortchanged, this models sticking up for yourself. If you received too much change, your words demonstrate honesty and communicate integrity around money. Let your children hear and see that you practice integrity with your money and they will learn to do the same with their money.

"They're filthy rich."

When you talk about money or rich people as "dirty," you perpetuate the myth that money is the root of all evil. Parent Talk of this nature creates a negative view of money in your child's mind. It brands money as evil.

In reality, money is a form of energy that enables us to have, create, exchange, and give. Some people may use it for negative outcomes. Most do not. Money itself is neither good nor bad. How people use it is what gives money its value.

Rid your Parent Talk of words and phrases that speak of money as nasty, ugly, dirty or bad. Help your children see money as the root of much goodness, kindness, and charity.

Focus on teaching your children how to use money for the betterment of the world.

"The charity jar is almost full."

Robert and Tammy Willow believe that giving is important. They believe that teaching their children about giving is equally important. That's why they began the charity jar in the first place. That's why it occupies an important place in their Sunday night ritual.

Each Sunday night, during their family meeting, the Willows distribute allowances to their children. The youngsters are invited to contribute some of their allowance to the charity jar. If or how much they contribute is up to each individual. Robert and Tammy model the importance of giving by adding a portion of their own money each week.

When the contents of the jar exceeds one hundred dollars, the family decides together on a charity to receive the money. One winter the Willow family bought gloves and donated them to the Salvation Army. On another occasion they adopted a whale. In the past three years they've purchased a winter coat as part of the Coats for Kids program, obtained and wore Lance Armstrong cancer bracelets, and made a donation to a local retirement ranch for abused horses.

Making a decision about where to send the contents of the charity jar provides a great lesson for children. Yet, the lesson does not end with that decision. The children help count the money. They watch as their mother writes the check. One of them addresses the envelope. Another adds the stamp and licks the envelope. All go to the post office to place their contribution in the drop box. All pray together as Mr. Willow asks that the money be used for the greater good of all concerned.

Giving has many dimensions, some obvious, some not. This family gave the money for the benefit of others, but in the process they gave themselves a deep sense of satisfaction. They gave other people's children hope while simultaneously giving their own children lessons on the importance of generosity and charity. They helped their children experience firsthand the important concept that giving and receiving are one. Charity clearly begins at home. Why not begin in your home by saying, "This looks like a jar. Actually, it is much more. It's a charity jar. Let me tell you about it"?

"**Money doesn't grow on trees.**"

Money does grow on trees—in the form of apples, oranges, cherries, pears, and lumber. Lots of livelihoods are maintained through these industries.

"Money doesn't grow on trees" is actually a sarcastic way in which some parents communicate, "I'm not an unlimited supply of money for you." Our suggestion: Skip the sarcasm and tell your children directly, "You will have to use your own money or find a way to earn more. I know you can handle it."

This is another sign that you're using sarcasm in your Parent Talk communication style.

Actually, you are a money magnet—attracting or repelling money through the beliefs, thoughts, and emotions you generate around money issues. Focus on lack and you experience greater lack. Focus on abundance and you attract more abundance.

How you talk about money attracts or repels it in your life. What you think about money pulls it closer or pushes it farther away from you. Your beliefs about money allow it to come to you or prevent its coming. You are indeed a money magnet, whether you know it or not.

For more information on how to teach the Law of Attraction to your children, see our book, *Teaching the Attraction Principle to Children*. It contains practical strategies for parents and teachers to help children manifest a better world. www.personalpowerpress.com.

Many children hear scarcity money messages

from their parents:

"There's never enough money."

"Hold on to it tightly. No telling when there will be more."

"I don't know where the money goes."

"I'll never have a nice car like that."

"DAD SAYS MONEY CAN'T BUY HAPPINESS SO I PLAN TO USE MINE FOR MATERIAL POSSESSIONS."

Why not use Parent Talk that teaches your children a belief in abundance? Help them learn how to be their own money magnets.

"Money is on the way."

"I'm so grateful that we have enough to give to others."

"Money seems to find you, doesn't it?"

"There it is again, money arriving right on time."

"Money always shows up with Divine timing."

If you think, believe, act, and talk as if you are a money magnet, you will help your children learn to do that for themselves.

"Wow!
I found a quarter.
The money just keeps
on coming."

Money comes to us in a variety of ways and at unexpected times and places. Finding a coin on the ground is a sign that the universe is continually active in providing money to those who are open to receiving it.

When you find a coin or when unexpected money shows up in your life from some other source, you have a choice. You can say, "Only a dime. You can't buy anything with a dime." Or you can say, "Wow! I found a quarter. The money just keeps on coming." Whatever Parent Talk you choose in these situations, know that you are helping form your children's money consciousness. You are helping them develop beliefs of abundance or scarcity.

Money that arrives in your life in even the smallest amount is a sign that more is on the way. Express your appreciation verbally so your children can hear your gratefulness and expectation of more to follow.

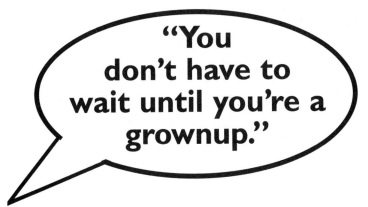

Children can make money, own a business, save money, invest in the stock market, and give to charities. Money is not just for adults. It's for anyone who has parents who are willing to help their children become financially literate.

Richard got bored during the summer and wanted to make a lemonade stand. His mother said, "Not today. It's too much trouble right now. You can do that someday later in the summer." She took him to get an ice cream cone instead.

Wendy also got bored during the summer, and she, too, wanted to make a lemonade stand. Her mother said, "Tell me more. I want to hear the what, why, where, when, and who that you've been thinking about." After a long discussion, she took her daughter shopping for lemonade supplies.

Both children learned important lessons from the results of their lemonade idea.

Richard learned . . .

1. An eight-year-old doesn't have much power.
2. It's hard to get your ideas taken seriously or even listened to.
3. You can earn an ice cream if you'll forget your latest idea and not bring it up again.
4. "Someday" means never.

Wendy learned . . .

1. Parents will listen to you and invest the time necessary to hear your thoughts and ideas even though they may not always agree with them.
2. It takes investment capital to begin a business. "Where are you going to get the money to begin this business?" her mother asked. "From you," the eight-year-old responded. "Not likely," her mother told her, "unless you want to pay me interest."

3. If you don't have money, other people will be happy to loan it to you if you're willing to pay them for that service. After hearing that she would be charged ten cents for every dollar she needed to get started, Wendy told her mother, "Maybe I have enough in my savings."

4. It helps to do some planning before you begin a business. "How much will I need?" Wendy asked. "Not sure," said her mom. "How many days are you going to do this and for how long? How much are you going to charge and where will you do it? Do you have a goal?"

5. Location is important. The first day of the weekend lemonade sale Wendy set up her operation in front of her own house. She had five customers in an entire afternoon. The next day she placed her table on her grandmother's front lawn during her garage sale. She sold out in two hours and had to restock.

6. In business you can help people and make money. Visitors to the garage sale were hot and thirsty. They appreciated the service that Wendy provided, and some tipped generously. She helped her customers stay cool and quench their thirst. They helped her earn forty-five dollars. It was clearly a win/win situation.

7. Always give people more than their money's

worth. In addition to a cold lemonade drink, Wendy provided napkins, a smile, and free refills. Most customers paid again when they got the free refill.

8. Credit isn't necessary. Wendy paid for the start-up supplies out of her savings. She paid in cash, sold for cash, and banked cash when she was done. A plastic card was not needed for any transaction.

9. It's important to give some back. Wendy placed 10 percent of her profits in the family charity jar after the completion of her lemonade adventure. She simply modeled what she had seen her parents do many times on Sunday evenings.

10. Cleanup is necessary. Just as Wendy was about to leave, her grandmother gave her a garbage bag to collect the paper cups and napkins that had been left in her yard. Wendy was tired and wanted to go home, but she realized cleanup was her responsibility.

Wendy and Richard had interesting summers. One child learned several economic lessons about starting a business. The other did not. One learned about responsibility, effort, persistence, and planning. The other did not. One learned that you can set a goal and achieve it. The other did not. One had a parent who realized that a lemonade stand offers incredible opportunities to learn life's success principles. The other did not.

"That vacation would cost too much."

"We don't have that kind of money."

"The dollars just aren't there."

Consider the following situation. Two fathers consider purchasing a new lawn mower at a local store. Both potential buyers have much in common. Their financial status and ability to pay are identical. They have the same amount of cash on hand. Even their desire and need for a particular lawn mower is identical. Each father is accompanied on the excursion by his children. Only the words they choose to use to describe the situation are different. Father A, in the presence of his children, examines the lawn mower, loves it, looks at the price tag and announces, "We can't afford it." Father B, in the presence of his children, examines the lawn mower, loves it, looks at the price tag and announces, "I choose not to buy it."

In each case, the situation is the same. The desire

is the same. The final decision is the same. Both fathers leave without the lawn mower. Only the words they used in front of their children were different. So what's the big deal? you may wonder. The big deal involves the words each father used and the pictures those words created for themselves and for their children.

Father A, who says, "We can't afford it," is using Parent Talk that creates a picture of himself as a person without enough money. He is creating a view for his children of a world of lack and limitation, of "not-enoughness." He is sending a message to himself and to his children that the family is not able to afford the purchase and that they are limited in money as well as in choices.

Father B, who made the same decision as father A, creates a different picture for himself and for his children by saying, "I choose not to buy it." His Parent Talk paints an image of himself as a person who is acting prudently—someone who has executed self-will and made a clear decision based on a desire for the lawn mower balanced with a desire to meet other priorities. His children are being exposed to an attitude of abundance coupled with choice. ("We can afford it and I choose not to.")

Father A leaves the store with his head down, feeling poor, powerless, and without choice. His children see his body language and sense the limited worldview demonstrated by their parent. Father

B leaves the store with his head held high, congratulating himself on a wise decision, feeling abundant and powerful. His children see his body language and sense the unlimited worldview communicated by their parent.

"Yoko's parents are really rich," Meggan told her mother.

"What do you mean by 'rich'?" her mother questioned, beginning a dialog that would increase both their understandings of what it means to be rich.

Is "rich" a large income? If so, how much is enough to be considered rich? How about a nice big house? How big does it have to be for a person to be rich? What about health? Can a person be rich in health or poor in health? And if a person has many possessions and is in poor health, are they rich?

When considering the issue of money, it's helpful to have conversations about the definition of rich. What does it mean to live a rich life? If you want a lot of *things*, what do you want them for? What qualities of life would they enable you to have? Can you measure a person's wealth best by looking at their bank account or in their heart? Maybe being rich is measured more effectively by what you choose to be as a person rather than by what you have.

When you hear, "They have a ton of money," "They are so rich," or "His parents have wealth coming out their ears," use those comments to begin a discussion on real wealth. Ask,

"What do you mean by 'wealth'?"

"He has a better job."

"We got a better deal on our house than they did."

"Sure they own a boat, but we have two horses."

These and similar comments teach children to measure their own worth by comparison. There is no need for comparison. We are all unique. Each person is unique and each family is unique. We are all enough.

Comparing does not serve any useful purpose. An inaccurate and inappropriate sense of superiority or inferiority is what usually comes from comparisons, especially when talking about wealth or money. Eliminate these kinds of comparisons from your Parent Talk. Accept where you and others are now without using that information to make judgments.

There is danger in verbally coveting your brother's—or neighbor's—TV, car, boat, camper, house, or swimming pool in the presence of your children. If you speak longingly of your neighbor's possessions or of the big flat-screen TV in the show room, your children strengthen their belief in the importance of things. They learn that material things are what one hopes for, strives for, and accumulates. This philosophy was aptly expressed on a T-shirt we saw recently. It said, "The one who dies with the most toys wins."

"What's the hook here?"

Your children are consumers. You don't think so? Doesn't matter. Business and industry know what you don't. Today children are increasingly being targeted as consumers by big business. And with good reason. Children in the United States ages four to twelve now spend over 24 billion dollars a year. And that's their own money they're spending.

Are you helping your children be aware of the marketing that is being directed at them? Businesses are actively working to manipulate your children into spending their money. They want it, and they're working hard to get it.

When you walk through the mall with your children, stop and look at window displays. Ask them, "What are they selling here? How are they trying to hook us?" When you watch a commercial on TV, ask, "What technique are they using to sell this?" Discuss advertisements in the paper. Look for words or pictures designed to get attention.

The following Parent Talk questions are useful discussion starters when building consumer protection in your children.

"How are they trying to get us to want this?"

"Who are they trying to sell this to?"

"What emotion are they trying to hook here?"

"Why do you suppose they use a celebrity to sell this?"

"What slogan are they promoting? Why?"

"What benefit are they pushing?"

"Are they trying to get you to hurry? How come?"

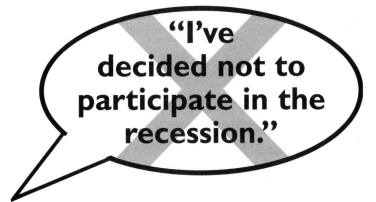

"I've decided not to participate in the recession."

The nightly news has been filled with negative stories about the economy lately: The stock market is down. We're in a recession. Could it be a depression? Maybe it will be a double dip recession. The unemployment rate is growing. The dollar isn't worth as much as it once was. Better invest in gold. Consumer confidence dropped again this month.

So turn off the TV. Stop putting all that negative energy into your mind and the minds of your children. News organizations catastrophize on purpose. They do that so you will continue to tune in to find out just how awful things are again today. Refuse to participate in the negative thinking. Refuse to participate in the recession.

Being in a recession is mostly a state of mind. Your beliefs about a recession create your present reality about the recession. You can't control the entire world economy, but you can control how you view it, how you interpret it, and how you react to it.

"I'm looking for a second job. I refuse to participate in the recession."

"We may change where we go on vacation and what we do there, but we're going somewhere. I refuse to participate in the recession."

"This holiday season we'll be making many of our gifts. And there will be some. Let's refuse to participate in the recession."

"There is someone who has less than we do. Let's share some of ours and refuse to participate in the recession."

"I'm going to be working longer hours. I refuse to participate in the recession."

Being poor is a frame of mind. It has more to do with how you think about wealth than with the state of your bank account. Refuse to create a recession in your mind. Refuse to pass on that negative thinking to your children. Refuse to participate in a recession.

SEX

Rochelle walked into the room to find the contents of her purse dumped on the floor. Her three-year-old son held up a tampon and asked, "Mommy, what's this?"

Veronica and Tim are uninhibited about nudity. They dress and undress in front of their young children regularly. Recently, Veronica looked up and noticed her five-year-old son staring intently at her naked body. "I'd better do something about this," she thought, "but what?"

Claude was sliding the last batch of muffins into the oven when his nine-year-old son interrupted with a question. "Dad, what's an orgasm?"

Ready or not, like it or not, Rochelle, Veronica, and Claude all found themselves in the position of sex educator. If it hasn't already, the same will happen to you soon. Are you ready?

Some parents attempt to avoid talking with their children about sexuality as long as possible. Others freeze up and break into a clammy sweat when it comes to answering sex-related questions. The bottom line is this: Sex and sexuality is a topic that your children want and need to know about. They're going to obtain sexual information somewhere. Do you want to leave their sex education to television or to their peer group? Do you want them getting their information in your home from loving parents or on the street from acquaintances?

The most appropriate answer to those questions

is clear. It is time for parents to reclaim their role as sex educator. In order to do that you will have to open up the discussion about sex with your chil-

"I'VE GOT TO TALK TO MY MOM. SHE THINKS THE STORK BROUGHT ME."

dren. You will need to be ever alert for teachable moments and be ready to talk and listen. Communication between parent and child is the key component in raising sexually healthy and responsible children. The Parent Talk phrases in this section will assist you in the process of being the sex educator your children really deserve.

"There is something I need to talk to you about."

"It's time for us to talk."

"There is something you need to know. Let's go in your bedroom where it's private."

If you're waiting to have *the talk* with your child, it's probably already too late. They have already developed their core beliefs about sexuality, where babies come from, sex roles, and the opposite sex. TV, the Internet, movies, and peers beat you to the punch. They got there first and won your child's ear. The best you can do now is work to catch up.

The days of having *the talk* with children are over. If you're still thinking about having *the talk* with your child, you need a paradigm shift. You need to scrap the outdated notion that one talk is all that's needed and begin a lifetime dialog that will give your children real information about sex and sexuality that will help them move through the stages of their life functioning sexually in physically and emotionally healthy ways.

Don't you dare wait to have *the talk.* Have lots of little talks throughout each and every developmental stage your child moves through. Begin today to assume your rightful role as the primary sex educator of your child, and do it on a regular basis.

"I thought you'd never ask."

If you're waiting for your child to ask about sex, you've probably waited too long already. Did your child walk up to you one day and ask, "Will you teach me how to use a fork and spoon?" or "What's that big bowl in the bathroom with water in it that swirls all around sometimes?" Probably not. What you did in those cases was grab the initiative. You looked for opportunities to teach about the fork and the spoon. You watched for chances to help your child learn about the toilet. And you taught without waiting for a question to get the ball rolling.

Do the same with sex. Look for opportunities to talk about sexuality. Don't wait to have *the talk.* That's not how it's going to happen. Your child is not going to walk up to you and say, "I want to have the sex talk now." Remember, by the time you're ready to have *the talk,* your child has already been listening to lots of sex talk somewhere else.

The goal is for you to support your children in becoming fabulous, wonderful, sexually rich people. This involves teaching them about taking care of and being responsible for their bodies with appropriate choices about nutrition, hygiene, teeth, hair, and skin. It also includes learning about gender, feelings, bodies, maleness and femaleness, relationships, love, intimacy, values, and communication. And it means giving them the facts.

Facts are important when it comes to teaching your children about sex. But talking about the "facts of life" is not enough. Healthy sex education includes teaching values, communication skills, and decision-making skills. It involves learning to respect yourself and others. Learning to respect your body as well as the bodies of others is another important dimension.

"This is embarrassing for me to talk to you about. And I'll do it anyway."

It's been said that it's easier to DO sex than to TALK about sex. For some parents that statement is right on target.

Many adults find it embarrassing to talk about sex, even with their partner. They believe that polite people don't discuss sex. They become nervous and apprehensive at the sheer mention of the word. Because of their fear and anxiety, they don't talk about sex with their children either. As parents, they avoid the role of sex educator of their children, postponing that important responsibility until their children have already developed many erroneous beliefs about sex and sexuality.

But wait. What we're recommending here is that your Parent Talk around this topic include much more than just the sex act. It's important that your communication with children about sex covers a much broader scope than simply how babies are made. Facts about how babies are made, how to not get pregnant, or how to protect oneself against sexually transmitted infections is a small part of the education children need about sexuality. Indeed, your responsibility as a sex educator goes well beyond giving facts about sex.

Sex education is about shaping an entire way of experiencing life. It's about helping your children learn how to experience themselves and experience other people. As sex educators, parents teach values and communications skills. They provide their children with decision-making strategies and practice various methods of problem solving. They dress appropriately for the occasion at hand and show affection toward their partner in the home and in public. They demonstrate tolerance for the lifestyle choices of others even if they don't agree with those choices.

Talking about sexuality is a crucial part of a child's development. Children start forming their attitudes about sex early in life. This learning is a lifelong process that actually begins at birth. A baby's attitudes about sexuality begin to form based on how they are held or touched.

As children grow, they learn from watching their parents. They observe how their parents show affection, act around people of the same and opposite gender, and respond to nudity. Children also form attitudes about sexuality through their exposure to TV, music, and magazines. Unfortunately, many myths about sexuality are perpetuated in the media and entertainment business. Therefore, it's critical for the parent to foster healthy attitudes and promote a better understanding of sex and sexuality. Sexuality is a facet of the human personality. It is a fundamental building block determining who your children are, how they treat themselves, and how they treat other people.

You don't have to be a sex expert or a doctor to assume the role of primary sex educator for your children. You are not a dentist, yet you teach your child to brush and care for his teeth. You are not a doctor. Still you teach your child how to take care of herself when she has a cold or is feeling sick. You are not a grammar teacher, yet you teach your child how to use words and structure sentences.

You don't need to know everything about sex to assume the role of sex educator for your children. Stick to the basics of what you do understand. Keep yourself informed as best you can. If necessary, learn right along with your children. Tell them, "I don't know the answer to that, but I know where we can find out," or "Let's see what we can learn about that together." Then search for answers as partners solving a puzzle.

"Go ask your mother."

"It's your dad's job to talk to you about that."

"Mothers know more about that."

Your child came to you and is asking you for help or information. Mom, if your son felt comfortable enough to ask his father the question, he would have. Dad, if your daughter felt comfortable enough to ask her mother the question, she would have. Don't pass the buck. Field the questions that come to you. They are being brought to you for a reason.

If you don't know an answer, say you don't know and together go ask someone who might. You can consult with the other parent later if needed.

"Aim your pecker in the middle of the toilet."

"Cover up your boobs."

"The ball hit him right in the family jewels."

Please use Parent Talk that reflects accurate terminology for body parts. Call a penis a penis, not a Willy, a worm, or any other slang term you perceive as cute. Breasts are breasts, not boobs, knockers, or titties. Testicles are testicles, not balls, nuts, or family jewels. And just for the record, the vulva is the outer part of a woman's vagina that we can see and the vagina is the inner part.

Children need to know what the body parts are called, how they work, and what differences occur between genders. Don't confuse the matter by making up cute words for important parts of our body.

If your child has a health problem, he can communicate with the doctor, teacher, relative, or coach more effectively if he knows the correct terminology to use. It's difficult to understand what someone is saying about the penis when you don't know what they're talking about. Let go of your anxiety about saying the correct word and get on with being the primary sex educator of your child at an early age.

"You're too young to talk about that. Ask me when you're older."

"You shouldn't be talking about that at your age."

"Ask me in about three more years."

"That's for older people to know."

One obstacle many parents face when preparing to talk to their children about sexuality is fear. They worry that giving their children too many details about a sexual topic too early will somehow distort their sexual development. Parents of young children worry that they will say too much and harm their children, while parents with adolescents and teens fear that talking about sex will lead to increased sexual activity in their children.

Parents who attend our workshop Parents as Sex Educators often inquire about what sex information is appropriate to give their children at different ages and stages of development. When parents feel secure and confident that they have the right information for the appropriate age, they feel more confident and secure in their ability to deliver that information. Confident parents help children feel secure about sexual issues, and that solid connection enables the children to make responsible decisions concerning the information they're given.

As you use the information below, remember that knowledge about sexuality is empowering for children. It is not harmful.

Birth to Age 1

During the infant years, hold, cuddle, love, and respect your child anyway you can. Work to create a bond of intimacy and trust between the two of you. Skin-to-skin contact is crucial to the creating of a bond. Take your shirt off and snuggle your naked baby. This applies to both parents equally. How you respond to your children when they are babies will influence how they respond to you later.

By the end of this stage children should:

- feel loved.
- feel respected.
- have a bond of trust and intimacy with both parents.

Age 1 to 2

The toddler stage is when children first notice a

difference between the bodies of boys and girls. It's normal for children at this stage to play with their genitals or express interest in the genitals of other children. This is a good time to talk to them about what they can do in public versus what they do in the privacy of their own home. Avoid responding in anger and scolding.

By the end of this stage children should:

- begin to notice the difference between the bodies of boys and girls.
- know that it's OK to play with their genitals.
- know that it's OK to express interest in the genitals of other children.
- know when is an appropriate time to explore their genitals.
- feel safe in the exploration of their bodies.
- know that they are good enough the way they are.

Age 2 to 3

Between the ages of two and three (the toilet training years) is a good time to talk about bodily function and to foster positive attitudes about body parts. How you react and respond may have the greatest impact on what your child learns during this time. For example, young children think that bowel movements are part of their bodies. If they are told that bowel movements are bad, they may feel that they are bad, too. This age is also a time to teach children about who can touch them and where and how to tell a parent or adult if they have been touched in a way that has made them uncomfortable.

By the end of this stage children should:

- have a positive attitude about bodily functions.
- have an understanding of bodily functions.
- know about "good touch/bad touch."
- know who can touch them and where.
- know how to tell a parent or adult if they have been touched in a way that has made them uncomfortable.
- know that they are lovable and why.

Ages 3 to 6

Between the ages of three and six is when gender differences (boy vs. girl) come to the forefront. Children during this time are attempting to understand what it means to them to be a boy or a girl. They are usually very open and honest about sex. They are curious, interested, and frank. Therefore, this is a good time to encourage children to ask questions. If by the age of five or six your child does not seem curious or ask questions, look for an opportunity to bring up the subject of gender differences and sexuality.

By the end of this stage children should:

- know the correct terms for body parts.
- know that they are in control of their own bodies.
- be introduced to the many ways to express love.
- know about choices and decisions regarding what to do with their bodies.
- know where babies come from.
- understand the concept of gender.
- be able to freely talk to their parents about sexuality.

Ages 6 to 10

Between the ages of six and ten is when children begin using sexual slang. This may start around age six as "bathroom humor." Their use of slang can progress to other terms they pick up from older children at school or from TV. Be aware of how you as a parent use similar terms so as to not send a mixed message. During this stage children usually want brief and direct answers to their questions.

By the end of this stage (age 10) children should:

- know about sexually transmitted infections (especially AIDS).
- know that different sexual orientations exist.
- develop a sense of self in relation to other

people.
- develop their own sexual identity.
- know about reproduction.
- understand how the male and female bodies differ.

Ages 11 to 13

Between the ages of eleven and thirteen adolescents may become apprehensive about bringing up the subject of sex. Their bodies are changing and developing rapidly during this time. Early in this stage parents need to talk to the young males about erections and "wet dreams" and to the young females about menstruation. Make sure that children also have accurate information about STIs (sexually transmitted infections) and the "right and wrong" reasons to engage in sex. An important statistic to remember is that by age twelve only about 5 percent of the adolescent population has engaged in sex, but by the age of seventeen that figure has increased to almost 50 percent.

By the end of this stage (age 12) a young adolescent should:

- know that sexual feelings are normal.
- know about methods of birth control.
- understand that sex is pleasurable and natural.
- know that sexual intercourse can result in a

baby.

- know how sexual diseases are transmitted, treated, and prevented.
- know that different sexual orientations exist and are a part of who people are.
- be aware of what changes to expect in their bodies, including menstruation and "wet dreams."

Ages 14 to 18

During the teenage years young people become sexually mature and may have strong sexual urges. This is also the age when many young individuals are having their first sexual experience. Teenagers should be given the opportunity to talk openly about issues of sex and sexuality. Important topics of discussion would be STIs, masturbation, sexual identity, samesex relationships, and myths and assumptions about sexual orientation. Teenagers should understand the appropriate use of sexual terms and be taught a respect for a broad range of sexual expressions so they can be sensitive to them.

By the end of this stage (age 18) a teenager should:

- be given the opportunity to talk openly about issues of sex and sexuality.
- understand the appropriate use of sexual terms.

- respect a broad range of sexual expressions.
- understand myths and assumptions about sexual orientation.
- understand the role of masturbation in their sexual development.
- understand how sex is used by many people to manipulate.
- understand appropriate expressions of their sexual desires.
- be aware of ways to manage their own sexual desires.
- understand the relationship of choices, decisions, and consequences.
- feel free to explore the world around them and their involvement in it.

Parents need to be sensitive to the developmental stage of their children and know how to present sexual material based on each child's individual development. While parents need to be concerned about how they present the material, keep in mind that children will not absorb any more information than what they can developmentally handle.

"A man's penis fits into a woman's vagina and plants a seed."

It is important to know where your child is developmentally when giving information about where babies come from so you can provide information within their field of understanding. If your four-year-old asks, "Where do babies come from?", and you respond by saying, "OK, you've got your fallopian tubes and some follicle stimulating hormone, some amniotic fluid and a uterine environment . . .," you're going to lose a valuable teaching moment. Give sexual information appropriate to the level at which your child is developmentally.

Look for children's books that talk about babies and bodies. As your children grow, use science and nature books that provide reproductive information as a natural part of the plant and animal kingdom. Use pictures and diagrams for adolescents to help them better understand the changes that are taking place within their bodies. Watch educational videos about masturbation, appropriate ways to put on a condom, and sex positions with your teenager. Discuss the material openly. Pause the videos and dispel myths while providing accurate information. Although the video material may be graphic at times, we are not recommending that parents use pornographic movies. Sexologists and certified sex therapists work closely with reputable companies to produce and distribute educational videos for parents, couples, and therapists.

For more information on how to access materials on sexuality or to speak directly to a sexuality professional in your area, visit the leading regulatory and certification board for sex therapists and educators at www.aasect.org, The American Association of Sexuality Educators, Counselors and Therapists.

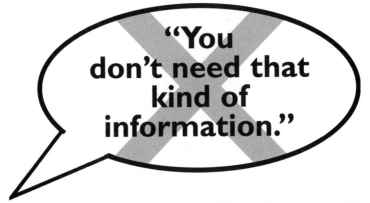

Many parents fear that talking about sex will increase sexual activity in their children. The fact is that knowledge about sex does not make children want to run right out and have it. Sexual knowledge is empowering. It helps children feel secure and gives them the tools they need to make rational, reasonable, conscious decisions.

No one worries that the information children get

"COACH FINDS IT HARD TO BELIEVE THAT I STARTED OUT AS THE FASTEST OF A HUNDRED THOUSAND SPERM."

in driver education classes will lead to more accidents. And no one worries that if children are taught about nutrition they'll immediately go out and hurt themselves by eating too much of the wrong foods. Don't worry that you might be telling your child too much about sex. Children will not absorb any more than what they can developmentally handle. The information that's out of their range of understanding will essentially evaporate into thin air. Children cannot hold onto information that is too sophisticated for their brains. This is true about many topics, not just sex.

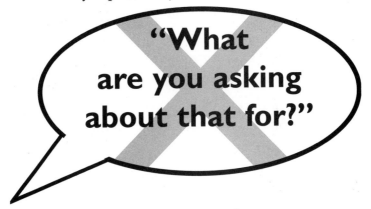

"Why do you want to know?"

"What are you going to do with that information?"

"What kind of question is that?"

If your three-year-old wants to know what's in your tampon box, do not overreact. Remember, this is a three-year-old asking the question.

To an adult this question is about a box containing an object that is placed inside a sexual organ, and therefore, indirectly, the question has something to do with sex. To the child, it's a question about a box and nothing more. Answer the question as if you were answering a question about a box of tissues. Say something like: "It contains a soft piece of tissue that women use," or "It's a little box that adults use to put stuff in from the drugstore."

If your ten-year-old son wants to know what's inside a tampon box, it's still a question about a box, and it's a great opportunity to further educate the child about women's bodies and women's menstrual cycles. Keep the information brief, making sure you don't lecture too long and ruin a chance for the child to return later for more information.

If your nine-year-old son wants to know what a "blow job" is, begin by asking him a few questions to clarify the question so you can be more accurate in your answer.

"What do you already know about blow jobs?"

"Were you talking about them at school with some of your friends?"

"Where did you hear about blow jobs?"

Avoid asking, "Why do you want to know that?" or saying, "Kids your age don't need to know about those things. Those are terrible words to say. Don't talk like that around here."

Give your son accurate information without chastising him for asking the question. Explain what a blow job is and tell him it's a part of having sex. For some people oral sex is only part of what they do for others in the beginning part called foreplay. Discuss appropriate times, places, and people to do that with. This is where you talk about how you feel about oral sex and clarify your personal moral position. Remember, many adolescents and teens do not consider blow jobs an act of sex. This is where you make sure your child understands that it is an act of sex and that sexually transmitted infections can be acquired this way.

"Thank you for asking."

"I appreciate your willingness to ask that."

"Thank you for taking a risk."

"That would be important to know, wouldn't it?"

Use Parent Talk that honors your child's effort in asking. Asking about sexual issues may not be easy for them. Affirm their risk-taking. Give them credit for inquiring and they will be more likely to ask in the future.

Ten-year-old Haim McCarty asked three pointed questions about contraceptives. His mother finally told him, "Stop asking so many questions." Haim got the message: Understanding is not important. He stopped asking.

If your children feel free to ask you sexual questions, you're doing something right. You have approached sex up to this point in a way that encourages your child to feel safe enough to ask. Good for you. Pat yourself on the back.

"What have you been hearing?"

"What do your friends tell you about that?"

"What parts are you sure of?"

"How would you answer a friend who asked about that?"

Adolescents and teenagers often claim to know everything about sex and aren't interested in what you have to say on the topic. If this occurs, switch gears and engage them in a discussion about what they know. Ask them to shed light on the topic for you from a teenage perspective. Once they begin talking, you will glean valuable information on what they do and don't know about the topic at hand. You may then be able to correct any misinformation without seeming to lecture or appear to be forcing your opinion on them. If nothing else, by asking for information from them you have begun a valuable dialogue and have kept the lines of communication open for future discussion.

Be willing to listen to your child and demonstrate that willingness by refusing to lecture and give information too quickly. You are on a fact-finding mission here. You will collect no facts if you do all the talking.

If your nine-year-old daughter asks you what a condom is, start by asking her what she knows about condoms and what specific information she would like to know. This will give you a reference point from which to provide more information. At nine, she probably doesn't need pictures or a demonstration. A simple explanation of the purpose and importance of using a condom will probably be enough. Let her know that when she wants more information all she needs to do is ask, just like she did this time.

Be honest with your answers. When children ask a question about sex, it's usually an indication that they've been thinking about it, need more information, and are probably ready to know. Your children will quickly learn whether they can trust the accuracy of your answers or not. If they feel they can't, they'll stop asking you their important sexual questions and turn to friends, TV, or magazines for answers.

"**Listen to what I read on the Internet today.**"

Stay open to the teachable moments that present themselves regularly. Those opportunities abound and you will find them if you look for them purposefully.

You can create many teachable moments by keeping a close eye on the news. Children are aware of what is happening in the news. They hear about it at school, on TV or the radio, in talking to their peers, and through overhearing your conversations. Use that information. Read the Internet article at the dinner table. Begin a discussion. Share opinions.

Notice billboards on the roadside, posters in the mall, and commercials on television. Use what your children are being exposed to and help them better understand the world in which they live. Debrief what is going on. Explain the hidden messages. Point out the sexual overtones. Correct any myths about sexuality. Confront any social injustices.

Interpret the event. Provide alternative points of view.

When your toddler is touching his penis, you have a teachable moment in which you can talk about accurate names of body parts or appropriate times and places to touch oneself. When your third-grader mentions gym class and how boys are better in sports than girls, you have a teachable moment in which you can talk about gender stereotyping. When your adolescent is considering going to the sixth-grade dance, you have a teachable moment in which you can talk about respecting other people's bodies. When your teenage daughter starts getting regular texts from boys, you have a teachable moment in which you can talk about love and relationships. Teachable moments are everywhere and happen regularly. These moments are your time to provide brief information about sexuality.

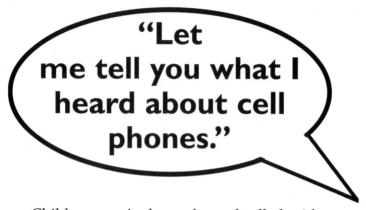

Children won't always be enthralled with your decision to seize a teachable moment. They may not want to talk about what you want to talk about, especially concerning sexual topics. On these occasions a conversation is not always necessary and an attempt to start one would only be forcing the issue, causing them to resist now and perhaps be reluctant to initiate important conversations later.

Simply state matter-of-factly what you heard or read. Then move on. "I heard that a kid who sends sex-related pictures on their cell phone can be prosecuted for distributing sexual material to minors and can be put on a sex offender registry with rapists and child abusers. Did you also know that they would be on that registry for over twenty-five years?" If you get no response, don't push it. There will be another day and another time. Many of them.

Teens will often claim they know everything already. You might hear, "I know," as a common refrain from your adolescent children. Don't let that stop you from providing them information. Without lecturing and rambling, tell them what you have heard or learned about the topic at hand. When they say, "I know," you can respond by saying, "Good. I'm happy to know you're aware of the legal consequences that are possible in a situation like that."

You just gave your child valuable information which they may or may not have known. And you did it in a nonconfrontational way that was brief and to the point. Move on and wait for another teachable moment. More are coming.

"I found a condom in the washer."

Occasionally a teenager will leave you an unintended clue about their sexual interests or activity. You may find a condom in a pants pocket, a note from a boyfriend on the bedroom floor, an explicit text message or a pornographic URL on the computer. In their own unconscious way, your teens are reaching out to you for more information. Do not misinterpret what is happening here. They are NOT asking for ridicule, condemnation, or punishment. They are asking, in their unsophisticated way, for guidance and assistance, not shame or blame.

How you received the information is not as important as what you do with it. There is no need for you to tell your son you found a condom in the washer or your daughter that you noticed a picture on her cell phone. They'll figure that out soon enough. Move past how you got the information to what they need now: information and guidance.

The discovered condom, text message, or birth control pills is a call to action. You are now being called to step up and actively take on the role of sex educator for your child. Your teen is asking you to help him or her meet a core need. Your main job is to identify the need that is being expressed and then meet that need with an empathetic and skilled response. Consider three areas of possible need: limits, values, and information.

It could be that the main need at this time is the establishment of healthy limits. Your teen may need you to set and/or reinforce age-appropriate limits. If porn sites are being visited on the computer, then parental blocks and pass codes need to be installed and adjusted regularly. If sexting is the issue, then cell phone limits are in order. When setting a healthy limit, say less and act more.

Perhaps you identify the main need in these and similar situations as one of clarifying values. Teens need adults to help them clarify the difference between opinions and facts. This may be a time when you determine that providing a clear definition and interpretation of the value system of your family and surrounding culture is in order. For instance, if you find a note that describes a dating practice that contradicts your family values, it may be time to bring that topic forth for serious conversation. The topic of boyfriends and dating would be worth discussing as you share how you feel about dating and what you consider age- appropriate dating behavior. Remember to be brief and avoid lecturing.

Maybe providing information is what is needed. Teens require an ongoing source of accurate information. They need factual knowledge about the human body, sexuality, dating, love and relationships. A condom in the pocket may indicate that your son needs more information about condom application and use, how to store a condom appropriately, or about other forms of birth control.

It is vital that you don't become overly emotional and act impulsively when your teens leave you clues about their level of sexual activity or knowledge. Take your time in identifying the need or needs to be addressed and look for teachable moments to provide the appropriate response.

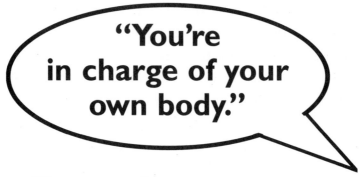

"It's your space."

"You get to set the boundaries of your own body."

"Other people get to set their boundaries, and it's important to respect them."

Communicating the "you're in charge of your own body" message needs to begin at an early age and continue until children leave home. When Aunt Bertha visits and immediately grabs your toddler and attempts to give her a big hug and kiss, intercede. Tell Aunt Bertha, "Bertha, we let each individual in this family decide whether or not they want to be hugged. You need to get permission from Sabrina or wait for an invitation. Thank you for respecting her personal space."

It can be frightening to a two-year-old to have some stranger (stranger to your child) come up to them, smelling of unfamiliar perfume, and invade their private space without permission, dispensing unwanted hugs and kisses. Protecting them now and honoring their personal space sets the groundwork for them to do it for themselves later. It sends a clear message: No one gets to be in your space without your permission.

Helping children learn that they are in charge of their own bodies relates to and is not limited to the topic of sex and sexuality. The "you're in charge of your own body" message is much broader.

A valuable lesson for children to learn at any age is how to be in charge of themselves. It is not a parent's job to be in total control of their children and tell them continually what to do or what not to do. It is a parent's job to equip and empower their children with the ability to make responsible decisions and choose responsible behaviors. Our job as parents is to make ourselves dispensable by gradually teaching our children how to take care of themselves, make choices that are in their best interests, and behave in respectful, caring, confident ways.

The "you're in charge of your own body" message can be delivered while teaching children to brush their teeth, eat healthy foods, engage in regular exercise, or get enough rest and sleep. Once children take ownership of their own mental, emotional, and physical health, they will be more likely to manage their sexual lives responsibly.

Telling adolescents and teens to "just say no" to having sex is a risky practice. First of all, most kids between the ages of thirteen and nineteen don't consider kissing, fondling each other's genitals, or even oral sex as sex. They engage in these intimate interpersonal interactions believing they are not having sex. Because of their narrow definition of what sex really is, saying no doesn't even enter their minds.

Telling kids to "just say no" without teaching them how to do that is like telling them to "just solve the math equation" without doing any direct teaching to accompany the declaration. If you want a behavior, you have to teach a behavior. If you want children to say no, you have to teach them how to say no effectively.

Teaching a child to say no involves direct teaching, practice, and debriefing. In includes when, how, and why to say no.

Give them the words for saying no.

"Please stop."

"I feel like I'm being pressured by you right now

and I don't like that."

"It's my body and I don't need a reason. The answer is NO."

"I'm comfortable with doing this, but not that."

"It's time to back off."

"I prefer to wait until I feel more comfortable."

"I choose to have a relationship with you that isn't focused on sexual activity."

"I'm not comfortable right now and I'd prefer doing something else together."

"If you're going to continue to pressure me about doing something I don't want to do, I'm going to leave."

"Please treat me like I'm someone you care about."

Talk about when you might use these words. Do you wait until you're in the back seat of a car or do you draw your lines well before that? When do you make this conscious decision? And when do you verbally make that decision known?

Practice using these words with your children by roleplaying. You be the other person and let them resist your advances. Change roles. Let your children experience saying NO many times before they are actually called on to say NO in a real-life situation.

"Boys are responsible for saying NO too."

It's important for boys to learn to set boundaries. Our society perpetuates the notion that boys should expand the limits of sexual boundaries and girls should make those limits more constricting. Boys are encouraged to be sexually adventuresome, as if it's some sort of conquest or rite of passage. Boys don't say no to sex. They're supposed to be the ones going after it. They aren't encouraged to explore feelings. They're encouraged to get as far as they can in their sexual conquests.

We may not teach boys to be sexually assertive directly, but the message comes through nonetheless. We joke about "getting to first base" or "hitting a home run" as if sexual activity is a game. We ask, "Did you score?" or "How far did you get?" We smile and give each other a high five when advances are proven fruitful. Trying to "get into a girl's pants" becomes the main focus of dating for many boys.

Our society is slow to encourage a boy to

explore his feelings and process what he really wants. We don't give him permission to say, "I prefer to wait until I feel more comfortable."

Teach your boys how to respect their own and others' bodies. Help them assume equal responsibility in the choices that a couple makes regarding sex. Teach them to respect the NO they hear from their girlfriend. And yes, teach them to say NO when their boundaries are violated or disrespected.

"Teaching children to ask questions of themselves as they contemplate sex will help them move from being unconscious about their sexual choices to making conscious choices. When they learn the technique of self-questioning, they learn to explore wants, needs and possible outcomes from a position of personal power. They take control and lessen the chance they will say later, "It just happened," or "I just got carried away."

Questions young people should ask themselves as they contemplate sex include:

Do I feel comfortable?

Do I feel pressured?

How do I want to feel?

Could I get hurt by this?

Is this the type of person I want to be?

How would I feel if a friend was doing this?

Is this the type of relationship I want to have with my girlfriend [boyfriend]?

What is my purpose for wanting to do this?

What do I hope to accomplish by having sex now?

Will this be an enjoyable experience for me?

How will I feel about it tomorrow?

Would there be a better time or place to do this?

Am I prepared to accept the consequences?

Does my rational mind agree with my hormones?

Self-questioning is a technique that can be applied to many situations in a child's life. When you teach your children to self-question, you are teaching them a process that they can use when any new or uncertain situation arises. The questions they learn to ask themselves as they contemplate sex can be applied to many important situations in their lives. You are teaching them to use their inner authority and activate a valuable life skill they can use for many years to come.

"Don't be touching that."

"Stop touching yourself."

Children explore, touch, and fondle themselves. How you react when that occurs and what you say about it sends important messages to your children that can last a lifetime. It's OK and even beneficial for them to explore and become familiar with their body. Do not punish and ridicule them for touching themselves. Instead, redirect them with statements that affirm and teach.

"It's OK to touch yourself when we're at home."

"When you want to touch yourself, you can go to your bedroom."

"A good time to touch your vulva is when you're taking a bath."

"Touching your penis is something we do in a special private area, not the grocery store. Let's talk about some places where you would be comfortable doing that."

A woman recently asked us at a workshop, "My

three-year-old touches herself in public. What do I tell her without teaching her that touching herself is wrong?" We suggested she frame touching herself as a positive thing for her daughter to do if it's done in an appropriate place. She could say, "We think touching yourself is fine, and it's OK if you want to do that in your room. We don't do it in the super-market or at school. It's just not the thing that people do with their bodies around other people. We do that in the privacy of our home or our bedroom."

In this situation you can use examples from everyday life to help the child better understand. "You know how we don't eat in synagogue, or we don't take certain toys to the restaurant? That's because it's inappropriate to eat in the synogogue and play with toys in a restaurant, so we wait and do those things at a different time." You can point out that there is an appropriate place to go to the bathroom when in public, there are appropriate times to run and be loud, and times to use a quiet voice. In the same way, there is an appropriate time and place to touch your private parts.

"Don't touch yourself there. That's dirty."

This common phrase is often directed at young girls who are experimenting with masturbation. The message that touching yourself is dirty can be extremely damaging to their sexual health. Through this choice of words, girls are often left with the impression that they themselves are unclean, rotten, or naughty. They become confused about what they are feeling in their bodies and how feeling *good* can be so *bad*. They grow up believing that masturbation is wrong and that women should not enjoy sex. They refrain from allowing sex to be pleasurable and bear enormous guilt when involved in any sexual activity.

We need to stop talking about masturbation, feeling pleasure, or having sex as if it is a terrible, forbidden thing. Our children need to learn that their bodies are fabulous and that other people's bodies are fabulous as well. We are all wonderful, sexually rich people and need to be treated that way.

"Masturbation is wrong."

Historically, masturbation has been stigmatized in this culture as having pathological origins and negative physical and mental health consequences. Not true. Sexologists and sex therapists know otherwise.

Masturbation promotes physical, mental, and sexual health by increasing our awareness of our sexual preferences, capabilities, and personal limits. It is a valuable part of helping individuals make responsible sexual choices. If your Parent Talk shames, ridicules, or chastises children for masturbation, you are rendering them less response-able and lessening their chances of living full, enriching sexual lives.

"Oops, sorry."

If you walk in and find your child masturbating, your reaction should be similar to that of walking in on someone when they're going to the bathroom or changing their clothes. Say, "Oops, sorry," and then walk out and close the door. If your child is masturbating with a friend in the room, start with "Oops, sorry" and add, "I'll be back in five minutes to talk to the two of you." Then walk out and close the door.

When you return, talk about how masturbation is normal and OK *and* it is meant for doing by yourself. Tell them, "In our house, we consider masturbation a private act that we do when we're alone. When you are here at our house, we ask that you respect our views on this topic."

You should also contact the parents of the child visiting your home and discuss what happened and how it was handled. Keep from blowing this out of proportion, and make sure the children move on to other, nonsexual, ways of relating to one another.

"Here's what we believe."

By all means, share with your children what you and your spouse believe about sex, marriage, relationships, morals, and personal responsibility. Do this verbally as well as demonstrating your beliefs by how you choose to live your lives. The morals and religious beliefs you have as parents are important lessons for your children. Be sure to include in your discussions why you believe what you believe. Also, allow them time to question and assimilate the information you give them.

When you communicate your beliefs, share those beliefs in context with what others believe. Help your children appreciate that there are people who view sexuality differently than you do. Help them understand the different points of view and why you believe the way you do.

Be careful not to make others wrong if their beliefs are different from yours. The goal is to help your children interpret the world through the lens of your religion and morals, not to ridicule, judge and condemn others.

"What they did was bad."
"She shouldn't have been wearing white."
"They should be ashamed of themselves."

This attitude reflects a belief that is based on a specific moral and religious point of view. There are some religious beliefs that include the concept that people should wait until after they're married to have sex. If you share that belief, by all means help your children understand how and why it fits with your preferred lifestyle. Yet, do you have to make others wrong if they don't hold the same belief? Can you not teach your children what you believe about marriage and sex without seeing others as bad or wrong?

Share your beliefs about sex and sexuality in accordance with your moral and religious background. Stop dispensing guilt and focus on the positive aspects of sex in your belief system. Avoid associating the words *bad* and *feeling wrong* with sex.

Sex is an important part of who we are in the context of every religion. Focus on the positive aspects of sex and drop efforts to shame children into conformity.

"Save yourself for the one you love."

Many parents use this phrase as a way to convince their teenage daughter or son to abstain from sexual activity. The intended message of the "save yourself for the one you love" communication is to not have sex now. The underlying and unspoken message is that sex is an expression of love, and if you're in love then sex is the best way to show it. Actually, sex is a very small part of the expression of love. Children need to see and hear love expressed in a variety of ways. The "save yourself for the one you love" statement, which firmly binds sex to love, brings increased confusion to the topic of love and raises many questions for adolescents and teens.

"So if I love someone it's OK to have sex with them?"

"What if I have sex with someone and find out that I don't really love them? Was the sex wrong?"

"How do I know when I'm in love?"

"Then why is having sex with your child considered abusive? That's someone you love, isn't it?"

"Why can't I have sex with my sister or brother? I love them."

"You're divorced from Dad and say you don't love him anymore. Was the sex you had with him wrong?"

The big question here is: "So if I love someone it's OK to have sex with them?" Adolescents and teens *truly* believe that they are in love with their boyfriend or girlfriend. From their limited experience and understanding of love they feel that they are *in love.* To them the phrase, "Save yourself for the one you love," seems to be giving them permission to have sex now.

This is a statement that many parents use to sway their teens away from engaging in sexual activity too early. It's an attempt to get them to wait until they are older. This approach rarely works. Kids don't care about this fact. In reality, many adolescents and teens find it gross to even think about older people having sex. So delete the "older is better" sermon from your Parent Talk.

Although this statement doesn't deter teens from having sex, it is true. Some of the most sexually satisfied people are those above the age of sixty. So if sex *is* better when you're older, then we all should wait until we're at least sixty before we partake. Have fun convincing anyone to do that, unless of course they're already sixty. In which case, what are they waiting for?

"People have sex for different reasons."

Do not leave your children with the impression that all people have sex to demonstrate love. While it's true that sex and love often go hand in hand and complement each other, it is also true that many people have sex for a variety of other reasons.

- Some people have sex because it feels good.
- Others have sex to prove that they're a grown-up.
- Some people have sex for money.

- Others use sex as a way of rebelling against their parents or the church.
- Some people have sex as a way to manipulate or control someone else.
- Others have sex to satisfy an addiction.
- And yes, many people have sex as a way to demonstrate their love or feel connected to their partner.

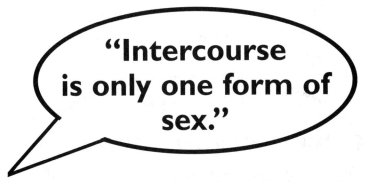

"Intercourse is only one form of sex."

Many adults fall into the trap of perpetuating the Clintonian definition of sex: "I did not have sex with that woman." They see sex as only involving intercourse. This is a narrow definition and creates a distortion for children. Sex includes a full, rich expression of our intimacy and connection with a partner. Sex is not just the act of intercourse or "getting it on." Many aspects of interpersonal interaction are sexual. Sex includes holding hands, caressing, making out, petting, cunnilingus, fellatio, erotic massage, masturbation, mutual masturbation, and tantric practices.

When we talk about these sexual interpersonal

interactions as something that merely leads up to sex (foreplay), children are left with the impression that sex is solely the act of sexual intercourse. This leads them to create distorted views and a narrow definition of sex.

Most teenagers, when asked to define sex, reveal a belief that oral sex (cunnilingus or fellatio) is not sex because vaginal penetration from a penis didn't occur. For some, if a condom is used or if ejaculation took place outside the vagina, then they didn't really have sex. For others, if anal intercourse took place, then they didn't really have sex. If dildos or vibrators were used to reach orgasm but no actual penis penetration took place, then they didn't have sex. If the girl didn't have an orgasm during vaginal intercourse, then she didn't have sex. The myths about what sex is and isn't abound among teens in today's world.

Among adolescents there is no clear consensus as to what really constitutes sex. As close as can be determined by sex researchers and sex educators, teenagers view sex as something that could create a baby. If there is limited probability that a pregnancy could occur, then to them it probably wasn't sex.

Help your children broaden their definition of sex by using Parent Talk that reflects that view.

"**Sex is enjoyable. It feels good.**"

Do not hide the truth from children. Sex is a fabulous, divine, life-affirming experience. Sex feels good and is fun, and it's OK to let teens know that. Hiding the fact that sex is enjoyable is a dishonest attempt to lead kids away from engaging in sexual activity.

Many parents worry that if children know sex is enjoyable and feels good, then they'll want to do it even more. That is simply not true. A major attraction drawing adolescents to want to experience sex is the intrigue of the unknown. By eliminating as much of the unknown as possible and helping them to understand what sex and the sexual urges they're having are about, you give them a solid base from which to make their sexual choices. Making the unknown known with honest information helps them realize that sex is a meaningful experience they are going to want to enjoy someday.

When teens internalize the notion that sex is supposed to be fun and enjoyable, you have given them an important measuring stick to assess their current experience. When they feel uncomfortable or uncertain, or when the experience isn't pleasurable or enjoyable, they're in a better position to stop and reevaluate what they're doing.

Thomas Haller, a certified Sex Therapist, frequently uses the following analogy when talking to teens about the joy of sex:

Imagine for a moment that you're at the mall looking for clothes. You go into a store you've never shopped at before. You immediately notice that the place smells like moth balls or a nursing home. The speaker system is playing old music that your parents listen to and the floor feels sticky. As you look around, an old woman using a walker keeps interrupting you and asking if you need help. Does that sound like an enjoyable shopping experience? Would you continue shopping at that store even if they sold stylish clothes? Probably not, because you know you can find a store that has the kind of clothes you like where you feel comfortable and can enjoy shopping. Sex is like that. You just know, for whatever reason, that it's not feeling right (peer pressure, alcohol, confusion, fear, coercion, a smell, sounds). That's a sign that you need to stop and "shop" somewhere else.

"Not true."

Children of all ages are filled with misinformation and untruths about sexual issues. Many myths abound and need to be corrected in order for young adults to live sexual lives that are based on fact rather than opinion and myth.

When you see some of the main sexual myths that are being promoted on TV, hear your child or one of their peers verbalize those myths, or notice behavior based on them, confront it. At these times the following Parent Talk is appropriate.

"Not true. Let me tell you why."

"The facts don't support that."

"That's one of the main myths about sex."

"A lot of people think that's true. It's not."

"Condoms are an effective form of birth control among teenagers."

Not true. Condoms are not an effective form of birth control among teens.

This statement would be true if adolescents and teens used condoms correctly. But they don't. Among the thirteen- to nineteen-year-old age group, condoms are only 65 to 70 percent effective. The primary reason for this is misuse.

Teens do not know how to use a condom effectively. And why would they? They are not being taught how to put a condom on, much less the importance of leaving room at the end for semen to collect. They are not informed that condoms with spermicidal creams are almost 10 percent more effective at preventing pregnancy than those without the cream. Most teens are not even taught how to store a condom safely.

With all due respect to "abstinence only" proponents, teens need to know about birth control. Yes, abstinence is the only sure way to prevent pregnancy. Teens need to know that, too. Teach them about abstinence. Yet, "abstinence only" is not working to prevent millions of teen pregnancies. To believe that abstinence will work for the majority of today's teens is wishful thinking. It's akin to the ostrich who keeps its head buried in the sand. Ever take a close look at an ostrich? There's another part of its anatomy that is vulnerably exposed.

Parents need to let go of the fear that their child will have sex if they talk about it. Having information does not increase a teen's involvement in sexual activity. It's time to stop preaching abstinence only and get on with the mission of providing a comprehensive understanding of sex and sexuality for children.

"If you're in love, sex will be great."

Not true. Resist making this statement to your children. It is Parent Talk that is not always true.

Think about your own life for a moment. You know there are times when sex is wonderful and times when it isn't all that great. Sometimes sex is painful, hurried, or disappointing. When those times happen, it doesn't mean that you are no longer in love.

The opposite is also true. You can have great sex with someone you just met and don't really know. It doesn't mean that you're in love. It means you had great sex. Sex does not equal love, and love does not equal great sex.

Sexual activity is only one way that couples demonstrate or show their love for each other. It's important to note that when a relationship is going well sex makes up about 25 percent of the couple's interactions. They're spending 75 percent of their interpersonal interactions being with each other in ways that have nothing to do with sex.

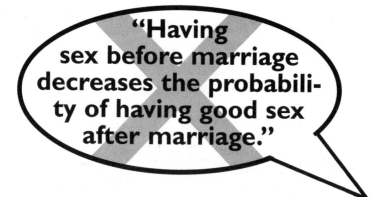

"Having sex before marriage decreases the probability of having good sex after marriage."

Not true. This notion is taught in some school systems across the country and is supported by proponents of abstinence-only education. There is no research or evidence to support this belief. This is a myth. It is simply an opinion and another misguided ploy to stop kids from having sex earlier in life.

We agree that many children are having sex too

early in life. We too would like them to wait longer until they are physically and emotionally prepared to handle it. In our attempts to help children come to that important conclusion for themselves, we need to be telling them the truth about love, sex and sexuality, not letting them become the victim of someone's persuasive attempt to manipulate them through unsubstantiated opinion, shame, or guilt tripping.

"Women want to be talked into having sex."

Not true. This is an extremely popular notion in the media. The woman says no two or three times and the man keeps pushing or asking. Eventually, she falls passionately into his arms. She has defended her honor enough and is now free to say yes and submit to the man's plea.

Be aware that this myth is being perpetuated in movies, on TV, and in books. If you haven't talked about this and dispelled this myth with your sons, they're learning that when a woman says yes it means yes. When she says no it means keep asking and eventually you'll get what you want. They're being taught that all they have to do is pay their due—buy dinner and a movie—ask endlessly, and eventually they'll get what they want. Boys are being taught that all they really have to do is outlast the girl.

This is not a message we want our boys, or our girls, to grow up believing. If you haven't already had this discussion with your teen, do it tonight.

Not true. The sexual behavior of both men and women is pretty similar. What is dissimilar is how that behavior is reported. The difference in how the reporting is done is due primarily to the level of social acceptance granted to each gender.

Men are more likely to boast of their sexual exploits, while women tend to downplay their sexual experiences. Women are frowned upon for talking about sex, and especially for stating that they want or like sex. Clearly, a double standard exists where sexual acceptance is concerned. This does a disservice to both young men and young women. It needs to end.

Women are not sluts, whores, prostitutes, or sex addicts because they like sex. Women are beautiful, fabulous sexual beings who enjoy the pleasure of sharing a sexual experience with their partner. They are no better or worse than men who enjoy the same sexual experiences. To have your daughter or your son grow up thinking differently is to ask them to live sexual lives based on mythology and a blatantly stereotyped view of sex roles.

Please refrain from using Parent Talk that perpetuates that double standard.

"Nice girls don't find sex all that much fun."

"Women just do it to please their husbands or to have children."

"Men are real animals in the bedroom."

"Just fake it and pretend you like it."

"It's the man's job to initiate sex."

Be careful how you talk about sex and sex roles with your children. You are planting the seeds of belief that can stick with them their entire lives.

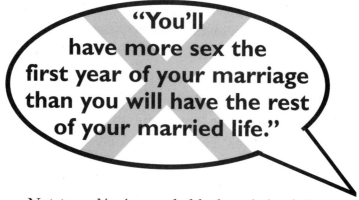

"You'll have more sex the first year of your marriage than you will have the rest of your married life."

Not true. You've probably heard the following quote. "In the first year of your marriage put a penny in a jar every time you have sex. Every year thereafter take a penny out of the jar every time you have sex and you will never be able to empty the jar."

This saying perpetuates the myth that you will have less sex the entire rest of your life than you did the first year of marriage. It's true that most couples have lots of sex in the first year of their married life. It's also true that as a relationship matures a couple may have less sex than they used to due to all the added stresses and responsibilities of marriage and raising a family. But this too is true: Over the course of their years together most couples will far surpass the number of times they had sex in their first year.

Children need to know that couples grow and change throughout the course of their life together. This phenomenon is called *relationship maturity*. Relationships mature as the people in them secure jobs, purchase a home, buy a car or two, have children, plan for the future, and increase their responsibilities. Don't let your son or daughter enter into a relationship, embrace marriage, and start a life with a partner believing, "You will have more sex the first year of your marriage than you will the rest of your married life." Clarify any misconceptions this phrase conveys and send your young adult into the world ready to mature into a loving relationship.

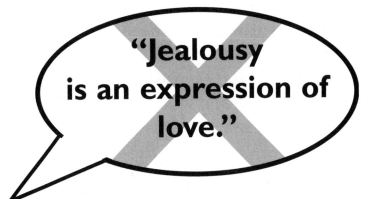

"Jealousy is an expression of love."

Not true. There are three types of love. Jealousy is not one of them. The three basic types of love are: eros, love of a partner; agape, love of God; and phileo, love of friendship.

By helping children understand these types of love and how to identify the many healthy expressions of love, jealousy can be seen for what it really is: the sign of a weak ego. Look for opportunities to point out how these three types of love are present in your children's lives. Love is expressed when taking care of someone in a time of need, volunteering or donating to a charity, listening to a friend, solving a problem together, giving a gift, spending time with each other, holding hands, and allowing someone else to express love in their own way. Demonstrate and articulate to your children the many ways love is expressed in your family and among your social groups.

Jealous people have a strong need to control the other person and often believe they need and deserve the full attention of that person. They feel lost, lonely, and frightened when the person of their "affection" is not solely focused on them. They feel diminished as a person if their "love" shows attention to someone or something else. Jealousy is a way an unloving person attempts to get what they want: attention and being taken care of. They often become angry and sometimes violent if they don't get what they want. Do not mistake this for love.

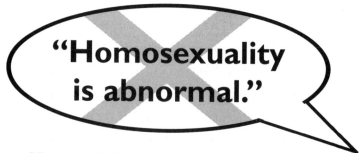

"Homosexuality is abnormal."

Not true. Left-handed people are not more emotionally disturbed than right-handed people. You are simply righthanded or left-handed. One is not better than the other. One (right-handed) is simply more prevalent than the other. One is not correct and the other is not incorrect. A person is who they are, right-handed, left-handed, or ambidextrous.

The same is true about sexuality. There are no clear-cut emotional or personality differences between homosexual and heterosexual people. There is no evidence in the research of psychiatry or psychology that homosexuality is any more of an emotional or personality dysfunction than hetero-sexuality.

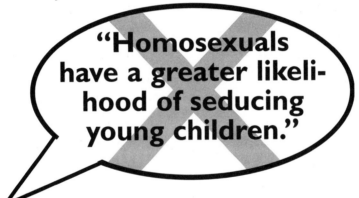

"**Homosexuals have a greater likeli-hood of seducing young children.**"

Not true. This is fabricated information based solely on fear and ignorance. This type of fear-based reaction has taken place throughout history as regions are populated with converging cultures. Over time, we learned that the fears we once held about a race or culture are largely unwarranted.

The myth stated above is misinformation. It too is based on fear. Actually, over 90 percent of cases of sexual abuse occur between a heterosexual man and a girl. End of story.

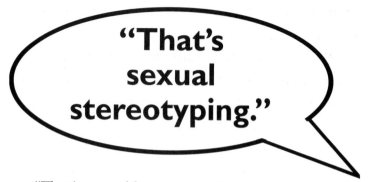

"That's sexual stereotyping."

"That's sexual harassment."

"That's racist."

"Words like that are hurtful."

"When you say that, you demonstrate an attitude of intolerance."

Children often use language that needs to be confronted directly. They make statements like, "That's so gay," or "You're such a fag." They use language they hear in school among their peers. They laugh at others who are not like them and call each other names that lead to continued misconceptions about gender, race, and sexuality. When this happens, parents and other adults who are present need to step in and correct the language misuse.

Labeling a certain type of behavior as gay or calling someone a dyke or lesbo is far more than just name-calling. Children need to know what their words mean and the effect their words have on others and the world around them. If parents don't correct the perception and the child's language patterns, the stereotype is reinforced and the myth about gender identity remains a constant in our society.

A carefully crafted lecture is not necessary when you hear stereotypical language. Keep your comments brief and to the point. Say, "That's sexual stereotyping," to draw attention to your child's statement. Follow that important piece of Parent Talk with a *because statement* that provides additional information.

"That's racist **because** the color of a person's skin has nothing to do with their abilities."

"That's sexual stereotyping **because** boys and girls act in a variety of ways regardless of their gender preference."

"That's sexual harassment **because** you're using your maleness to influence that girl's decisions."

"That's hurtful **because** you're making an assumption about that person's character."

When parents ignore their children's inappropriate statements, the children are left with the impression that it's OK to say those types of things. It's not OK, and it's a parent's responsibility to confront their children when sexual stereotyping takes place.

"A woman's place is in the home."
"Asians are terrible drivers."
"Big boys don't cry."
"Women are so emotional."
"White men can't jump."
"Boys are better at sports."
"Gay men are weak and feminine."
"Mowing the grass is a man's job."

The above statements and others like them perpetuate stereotypical myths and provide inaccurate information about gender and race. Men cry, cook, and clean the house and it has nothing to do with their being gay or straight. Women run businesses, fight in the army, and mow the grass because that is who they are and how they choose to be.

The messages that your Parent Talk communicates concerning tolerance and acceptance are subtle and yet extremely powerful. They shape how children see the world and the people in it. Your children are learning a great deal about sexuality by what you say to them that reflects a gender bias or an acceptance of a specific gender role. Through your words they learn about bigotry and prejudice or about love and grace. How you talk to your children about the world in which they live and the people they encounter along the way influences their view and affects their experiences.

Be mindful of the words you use and the actual message you want to impart. Take every opportunity to correct your children's misuse of words that may perpetuate an unhealthy outlook toward themselves or others.

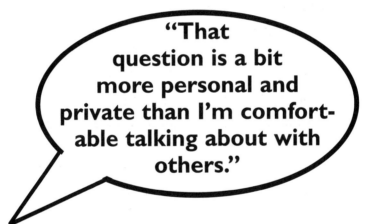

"That question is a bit more personal and private than I'm comfortable talking about with others."

Sooner or later, in their search for more sexual information and understanding, your children will ask a question about your personal sex life. What form that question takes you can't know ahead of time. You can't predict at what age it will arise. How many personal questions they ask will vary among children. But get ready. The questions will come.

"Do you and Mom have sex?"

"Do you like sex?"

"How often do you do it?"

"Did you do it before you met Dad?"

"Did you do it before you had me?"

"If you don't want to have any more kids, why do you still do it?"

You don't have to answer questions that you're not comfortable answering. An important lesson for your children to learn is that social norms exist around asking questions of a personal nature. Personal privacy needs to be respected. And that includes yours.

Suggested Parent Talk responses to questions that are personal and exceed your comfort level include:

"I'm uncomfortable answering that question completely for you right now, but I will tell you this . . ."

"I don't want to influence your decisions about sex by telling you what I did or didn't do."

"How would knowing that help you with the choices and decisions you're making about sex?"

"My personal sex life is private, but I'll tell you what I believe in general."

"What happens between your mother and me needs to stay with your mother and me. We respect each other's privacy in this area. Tell me why you want to know and maybe I can give you some information that will help."

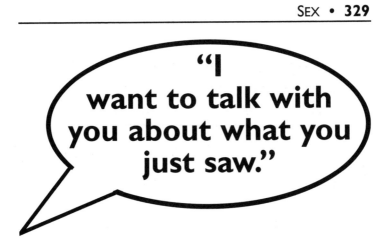

Don't be surprised if someday you get surprised. Of course you know enough to lock the door when you have sex. Yet, passion can arise quickly at times, and thinking logically that there are children in the house, the door needs to be locked, or we better not get caught can get in the way of a hot moment.

So what do you do if you get walked in on during the private act? What do you say to this child in the moments that follow? First, say nothing. Your first step is to watch closely how the child reacts. She may not say or do much about it. If that's the case, you don't say or do much about it either, other than locking the bedroom door and being more cautious. If the child asks questions, answer them according to her age level and understanding. She may simply ask, "What are you guys doing?" Respond, "We were being close and snuggling, as we like to do sometimes."

Either way, don't make a big deal out of it. The incident will not scar her for life. In fact, the more casual your response, the less likely she is to remember.

One Last Word

Consider parenting with the end in mind.

What is the end? What is the goal that you want to accomplish while raising your children? What do you want the end product to look like? If you are similar to most parents you want children to grow increasingly toward becoming responsible, caring, conscious adults. You want them to be personally responsible, decisionally literate, compassionate, honest and confident. You want them to be capable and wise with money, sexuality, relationships, and personal power. You want them to fully mature into what they are capable of becoming, taking responsibility for the choices and direction of their lives as they grow.

There is no way you can help your children leap from where they are today to the end product you desire. There is only a variety of little steps that lead in that direction. Some of the steps you can use are on the preceding pages. These verbal skills will help you reach the end you desire. You know which ones fit you and your family. You know which one you can begin to use today.

Why not begin today with a verbal skill of your choice? Invite your children to take another step in their growth toward being a conscious, compassionate, human being.

In addition to helping your children, the verbal skills presented in this book can help *you* change your parenting life. By finding and using the language you need to empower your children, you will empower yourself. By choosing language patterns that help your children feel connected, you will increase your personal bond with them. By speaking honestly and directly, you will increase your own level of integrity. By indentifying and implementing the verbal skills in *Parent Talk Essentials* that fit with your core beliefs and family values, you will move closer to becoming the parent you always wanted to be.

Beyond that, the verbal skills contained in this book can help you alter your family tree for generations to come. What you learn and use here will likely be learned and used by your children and in turn by your grandchildren. Your legacy as a parent who helped raise responsible, caring, conscious children can be passed on and lived by family members for years to come.

Here's to you, your children, and your grand-children. Let us begin.

ABOUT THE AUTHORS

Chick Moorman

Chick Moorman is the director of the Institute for Personal Power, a consulting firm dedicated to providing high-quality professional development activities for educators and parents.

He is a former classroom teacher with over forty-five years of experience in the field of education. His mission is to help people experience a greater sense of personal power in their lives so they can in turn empower others.

Chick conducts full-day workshops and seminars for school districts and parent groups. He also delivers keynote addresses for local, state, and national conferences.

He is available for the following topic areas:

FOR EDUCATORS

- Motivating the Unmotivated
- Achievement Motivation and Behavior Management through Effective Teacher Talk
- Celebrate the Spirit Whisperers
- Teaching Respect and Responsibility
- Cooperative Learning

FOR PARENTS

- Parent Talk: Words That Empower, Words That Wound
- The Only Three Discipline Strategies You Will Ever Need
- The 10 Commitments: Parenting with Purpose
- Empowered Parenting

If you would like more information about these programs or would like to discuss a possible training or speaking date, please contact:

Chick Moorman
P.O. Box 547
Merrill, MI 48637
Telephone: 877-360-1477 (toll-free)
Fax: 989-643-5156
E-mail: ipp57@aol.com
www.twitter.com/chickmoorman
www.facebook.com/chick.moorman
Websites: www.chickmoorman.com and
www.uncommon-parenting.com

Thomas B. Haller, MDiv, MSW, ACSW, DST

Thomas Haller is the chief parenting and relationship correspondent to WNEM TV 5 (CBS affiliate), MY5 TV, and WNEM News Radio 1250AM. He has been the weekly radio personality for over five years on Mid-Michigan's number one radio station WIOG 102.5 FM. Thomas is also the regular guest host of Health Line on WSGW AM790/100.5 FM. He has been a featured guest on over 150 radio shows, including such notable programs as *Oprah Radio, Playboy Radio* and *The World Puja Network.*

Thomas is a parenting and relationship specialist, the coauthor of five highly acclaimed books, a psychotherapist maintaining a private practice (for 20 years) as a child, adolescent, and couples therapist, a sex therapist, and a chronic pain counselor.

Thomas has a Master of Divinity degree, a Master of Social Work degree, and a doctorate in Child and Family Studies. He has extensive training in psychotherapy with children and couples. He is a certified EEG biofeedback technician, an AASECT certified diplomate of sex therapy, and a certified sports counselor.

In addition, Thomas is the founder and director of the Healing Minds Institute, a center devoted to teaching others to focus and enhance the health of the mind, body, and spirit. He is president of Personal Power Press, Inc., a small publishing house committed to providing parents and educators with practical material for raising responsible children. Lastly, Thomas and his wife Valerie maintain a not-for-profit 501 (c) (3) organization, Healing Acres, an equine retirement ranch enabling aged horses to live out their lives in a low-stress environment.

He is available for workshops, seminars, student assemblies, and commencement speeches.

Website: www.thomashaller.com

Twitter: www.twitter.com/tomhaller

LinkedIn:

http://www.linkedin.com/pub/thomas-haller-m-divlmsw-dst/1a/8/868

Facebook: www.facebook.com/thomas.b.haller

Blog: www.uncommon-parenting.com

Email: thomas@thomashaller.com

OTHER BOOKS AND PRODUCTS

www.personalpowerpress.com

For Parents

PARENT TALK: How to Talk to Your Children in Language That Builds Self-Esteem and Encourages Responsibility, by Chick Moorman ($15.00)

THE ONLY THREE DISCIPLINE STRATEGIES YOU WILL EVER NEED: Essential Tools for Busy Parents, by Chick Moorman and Thomas Haller ($14.95)

TEACHING THE ATTRACTION PRINCIPLE TO CHILDREN: Practical Strategies for Parents and Teachers to Help Children Manifest a Better World, by Thomas Haller and Chick Moorman ($24.95)

THE 10 COMMITMENTS: Parenting with Purpose, by Chick Moorman and Thomas Haller ($19.95)

THE LANGUAGE OF RESPONSE-ABLE PARENT-ING, audiocassette series featuring Chick Moorman ($39.50)

PARENT TALK FOCUS CARDS, by Chick Moorman ($10.00)

THE PARENT TALK SYSTEM: The Language of Response- Able Parenting, Facilitator's Manual, by

Chick Moorman, Sarah Knapp, Thomas Haller, and Judith Minton ($300.00)

DENTAL TALK: How to Manage Children's Behavior with Effective Verbal Skills, by Thomas Haller and Chick Moorman ($24.95)

For Couples

COUPLE TALK: How to Talk Your Way to a Great Relationship, by Chick Moorman and Thomas Haller ($24.95)

For Educators

SPIRIT WHISPERERS: Teachers Who Nourish a Child's Spirit, by Chick Moorman ($24.95)

TEACHER TALK: What It Really Means, by Chick Moorman and Nancy Weber ($15.00)

TEACHING THE ATTRACTION PRINCIPLE TO CHILDREN: Practical Strategies for Parents and Teachers to Help Children Manifest a Better World, by Thomas Haller and Chick Moorman ($24.95)

MOTIVATING THE UNMOTIVATED: Practical Strategies for Teaching the Hard-to-Reach Student, audio seminar featuring Chick Moorman ($95.00)

Qty.	Title	Price Each	Total

Subtotal		
Tax MI residents 6%		
Shipping and Handling (see chart below)		
Total		

Please add the following shipping & handling charges:
$1 - $15.00 — $4.95 $15.01 - $30.00 — $5.95
$30.01 - $50.00 — $6.95 $50.01 and up 15% of total order
Canada: 20% of total order. US funds only, please.

Ship To:

Name: _____

Address: _____

City: _____ State: _____ Zip: _____

Phone: _____

❑ **American Express**   ❑ **Discover**   ❑ **VISA**
❑ **MasterCard**   ❑ **Check/Money Order**
(payable in US funds)

Card #_____-_____-_____-_____

Expiration Date _____/_____

Signature_____

PERSONAL POWER PRESS, INC.
P.O. Box 547, Merrill, MI 48637
Phone: (877) 360-1477 - Fax: (989) 643-5156
E-mail: customerservice@personalpowerpress.com
www.personalpowerpress.com

East Smithfield Library

3 2895 00126 7595

NEWSLETTERS

Chick Moorman and Thomas Haller publish FREE
e-mail newsletters for parents and educators.
To subscribe to either of them,
e-mail <u>customerservice@personalpowerpress.com</u>
or visit <u>www.personalpowerpress.com.</u>

BLOG

Uncommon Parenting Blog -
<u>www.uncommon-parenting.com</u>

```
649.1  Moorman, Chick
MOO

     Parent talk essentials:
     how to talk to kids
     about divorc
```